The Dance of Love
My Life with Meher Baba

Front cover painting by Dot Lesnik

Quote from *The Dance of Shiva* excerpted from a publication of The Asia Publishing House of Bombay and Calcutta.

ISBN: 0-913078-40-9

Library of Congress Catalog Card Number: 80-53859

Printed in the United States of America

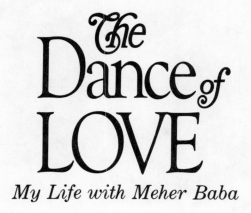

The Dance of LOVE

My Life with Meher Baba

MARGARET CRASKE

Sheriar Press

Meher Baba   *Cannes, France*   *1937*

*I*n the night of Brahma, Nature lies inert and cannot dance until Shiva wills it. He rises from His rapture and, dancing, sends through inert matter pulsing waves of awakening sound. And lo! matter also dances, appearing as a glory round about Him. Dancing, He sustains its manifold phenomena. In the fullness of time, still dancing, He destroys all forms and names by fire, and gives new rest.

This is poetry, but nonetheless science.

from The Dance of Shiva

Introduction

When Meher Baba first arrived in the West in 1931, His purpose was to contact, gather and train a small group of persons who were to become His closest Western disciples. Over the next 50 years, through an extraordinarily diverse range of activity, His love touched new depths in the hearts of His many followers and awakened in thousands of people all over the world a profound longing for union with God. But in 1931, as *The Dance of Love* opens, the scene is London and the cast of players a diverse group of strong-willed individualists gathered together by the drawing power of Meher Baba's silent call.

The stories that compose *The Dance of Love*—told with wit, warmth and love—follow Margaret Craske's relationship with Meher Baba from 1931 to the late 1960s when He dropped His body and left to His lovers the inner contact which He had told them was all-important. At the time of her momentous initial meeting with Meher Baba, Miss Craske had extended a noted career as a ballerina with the Ballets Russes during the days of Diaghilev and Cecchetti into ownership of a flourishing school of ballet in London, and was teaching for the Sadler's Wells Ballet Company (later the Royal Ballet) and choreographer for the Carl Rosa Opera as well. Years later, when Meher Baba asked her to go to America in 1946, she taught for American

Ballet Theatre, then for many years was assistant director of the Metropolitan Opera School of Ballet, and now teaches at the Manhattan School of Ballet.

It was Margaret Craske who opened the door for Meher Baba when He first arrived at the London home of Herbert and Kitty Davy's parents to begin His mission to the West. She saw Him at that moment as "a vision of gentleness, grace and love that touched the heart immeasurably." Before that first day was out, she says, "I only knew that from that moment, whatever rough treatment He may have afterwards handed out, there has never been a moment's doubt as to His being the embodiment of Love and Life."

Meher Baba came often to the West in those early years to share His company with His disciples. There were meetings first at East Challacombe in Devonshire, where Meredith Starr, who had initially contacted Baba in India, had established a spiritual retreat. Then He called them to other places, to Cannes, to Portofino and Santa Margherita, to Paris and to Lugano and Zurich, and finally to India. Told with vivid detail, great fun and simple warmth, Miss Craske's stories richly evoke the atmosphere of these early honeymoon days with Meher Baba.

The majority of Miss Craske's stories take place, however, in India, covering the Western disciples' first visit in 1936-37 at Nasik as well as tales from 1939-46, during which time Miss Craske managed, with a sharp wit and against all odds, to get to India as most of the Western world was bracing for a second world war. There are wonderful images here of the ways Meher Baba worked with His disciples, bringing together East and West in a manner that would have been very puzzling to Rudyard Kipling and other British inhabitants of India. There are perceptive portraits of some of the American and British people drawn into Baba's orbit in those years. And there is a special preservation of Meher Baba's sense of humor and the way he used to teach his followers "to take God seriously and life lightly."

The Dance of Love moves on to short stories of Baba's visits to the United States in the 1950s, with touching portraits of a few of the people who met Him then, ten years before the 1960s' flower children made looking for gurus, God and nirvana an American passion.

It is in fact the time span of Miss Craske's 50-year relationship with Meher Baba that forms the intrinsic value of this book, for those 50 years have provided her with insights and perceptions impossible to gain otherwise. She passes on her observations with a simple honesty that states the case exactly as it was, without embellishment: the periods of joy and fun, the times of hard work and frustration, the slow coming to an understanding of flexibility, naturalness and staying power required of those who would even approach the Spiritual Path.

But most of all, this work evokes for us to treasure the breathtaking atmosphere that swirled around Meher Baba, and the simplicity and directness of His relationship with some of His closest disciples.

Ann Conlon
Myrtle Beach, South Carolina

March, 1980

Foreword

These are some of the stories which show how Meher Baba the Beloved worked with His disciples in His great work of Awakening. Since it is true that after being told the same story usually returns to the teller mutilated and trimmed up so that it has quite a different meaning, I have therefore tried to stick to those with which I was personally associated or am fairly certain of their exactness and origin.

The stories start from His arrival in the West in 1931, His gradual bringing together of disciples from both sides of the Atlantic and the final joining of His Eastern and Western disciples.

The differences in social structure in the different places were, through Meher Baba's loving Awakening processes, faced and finally accepted. They did, however, at first cause much surface trouble. Some of these processes were painful; but the pain passed and each time it could be more clearly and beautifully experienced that Baba did not just love. He was Love.

Margaret Craske
Myrtle Beach, South Carolina

August, 1980

Contents

The Early Years

The Nasik Period

The War Years

In America

The Early Years

*I have come not to teach,
but to awaken.*

MEHER BABA

First Order

The day that Meher Baba arrived in London in 1931 on His first visit to the West seemed possessed of an unreal quality, as if every moment of life had been leading up to this day when the God-Man was coming to visit us. Yet at the back of this was a fear that perhaps, after all, those who had met Him were mistaken. There had been others claiming the Avataric role.

It was arranged that Baba should spend the first night in the one-time nurseries at the top of the Davys' house in Earl's Court and go on to Meredith Starr's place in Devonshire the next day. A group of people, including Kitty Davy, went to the station to meet Him, and I was asked to stay and greet Him at the house.

Just before the time for His expected arrival, the telephone rang. I answered it and there on the other end of the line was Herbert Davy. His voice was excited and had a touch of uplift in it. He said, "You don't know what has arrived. The most wonderful person you can imagine. And He sends you a message. You are to go round the house and close every door you find open. And then you must answer the front door yourself."

I did not, of course, realize that this was my Master's first order to me. In fact I did not know that He was my Master. But, fortunately, I told Herbert that I would do as Baba wished.

I nervously descended to the basement and shut the door, closed doors to rooms in which I heard voices, and in fact behaved in a strange house in an unforgivable manner. As soon as I had finished this odd performance, the bell rang and I opened the front door. And there at the bottom of the steps stood the most appealing figure that one could ever hope to see. No sign of power. Just a vision of gentleness, grace and love that touched the heart immeasurably. He came up the steps, gave me a passing glance, and, accompanied by Meredith, Chanji and others, went up the stairs to His room. I remained in the hall. A few minutes later Meredith came down the stairs and said very grandly, "Meher Baba wishes to see you."

Overcome by nervousness, I said, "Wouldn't He like to see somebody else first?"

Meredith looked at me sternly and said, "Meher Baba wishes to see you."

I accordingly turned and climbed three flights of stairs to the most important moment of my life, the meeting with my Master.

He was seated quietly in a chair, and He signed to Chanji to bring another chair and place it facing and close to His. He then beckoned me to sit there. For a moment or so there was intense quiet, and then I had a strong feeling that it was important to look into His eyes. Courage came and I did so, looking in deeply, deeply, as far as I could. I have nothing to say about what I saw. In fact, I don't know. I only know that from that moment, whatever rough treatment He may have afterwards handed out, there has never been a moment's doubt as to His being the embodiment of Love and Life.

A Lesson Through Humor

After His arrival in the West in 1931, Meher Baba went to East Challacombe to find that although Meredith Starr had done excellent work in introducing Baba to the West, his arrogance had not allowed him to relinquish his position as the orderer of events. Instead, he went on giving orders to the assembled guests. I do not mean household orders about mealtimes, bath water, etc.—they were admissible—but orders that should have come only from the Master Himself.

For example, Meredith would insist that at certain times everyone should retire to a quiet spot and meditate. Since one of the most powerful meditations is on the personal form of the Master, it seemed that just being with Baba met the case better than regular meditation for us. In any event, it was quite impossible to withdraw one's mind from this Vessel of Love, who had miraculously arrived in our lives, and we were, as well, quite untrained in the valuable exercise of meditation. Baba did not say anything to Meredith, but with much humor showed this to some of us.

One sunny afternoon the order came from Meredith for everyone to retire and meditate for one hour on some subject that he suggested. A few of us, who afterwards became close disciples of Baba, went to the bedroom we were sharing and settled down to do our best.

After a short time the door opened and in came Baba, looking delighted and signing to us not to speak. He tiptoed across the room to the open window, and everyone followed happily. Looking out, we saw Quentin Tod in shorts, his back bare, sitting cross-legged on the lawn. His back was to the window and he was doing his best to meditate. A look of mischief came into Baba's face. There was a bowl of lump sugar on a small table, and He took a piece in his fingers and threw it accurately onto Quentin's spine. Quentin quivered with indignation. He was working hard. This was too much. With great control he did not move or turn to see who was doing such a dastardly thing.

A minute or two later Baba repeated the performance. This time the spine looked as though it would dislocate itself with annoyance, but again Quentin remained in the meditation position.

He could not, however, stand a third attack. He sprang furiously to his feet and turned, obviously with the full intention of annihilating the culprit, but on seeing Baba and the laughing group in the window he stared incredulously, and then laughed and came to join the meditation on Baba with Baba.

That was the first hint we had that there was only one person whom we should obey, and later on, as the years went on, there were certain meditations that we did under Baba's orders.

First Dance Adventure

B aba spent His first night in England at the Davys' house in Earl's Court and the next morning went down to Meredith Starr's farmhouse in Devonshire. Meredith, under Baba's orders, had opened the farmhouse as a retreat where those interested in Him could go to meditate and hear about this then unknown spiritual figure.

The farmhouse did a wonderful job. It was through this obscure and quite wild place that Baba made His early connections with England and America.

On this first evening in London, Baba spoke to me about going to East Challacombe while He was there. I said that I was running a ballet school in London and that it was impossible to leave. I had no idea that being with a Master meant obedience regardless of anything. In fact, at that point, the idea of being a disciple had not entered my head. Baba turned on me pretty sharply and spelt out on His alphabet board, "You are My disciple, of My circle, and you must do as you are told," and although I had no idea of the meaning of this order, I arranged for someone to do my work and a few days later went to East Challacombe.

Meredith had collected a great many persons to meet Baba. All kinds. Some who were searching for the truth, some who had been mixed up with black magic, some who were curious and a few who turned out to be of Baba's circle. During this first visit to England, He found all of His close English disciples, including Quentin Tod, Charles Purdom, Delia de Leon, Herbert and Kitty Davy, Mabel Ryan, and others.

It was a beautiful experience to be with Baba for the first time. He was unbelievably beautiful, not just physically, but lighted up with a spiritual beauty.

One afternoon we were sitting with Baba on a steep hillside. A very craggy place, not a piece of smooth ground anywhere. Suddenly Baba's face lighted up as if He had had a world-shaking inspiration, and He spelt on the alphabet board, "Margaret shall dance for us." I was horrified. First, there did not seem to be a flat piece of ground anywhere on which one could dance. Second, I had on clumping country boots and a tightish, thick tweed skirt in which it was impossible to lift a leg or step out; and third, I was convinced, rightly, that I should make a fool of myself. And I wish to say that in all the years I was with Baba I never did dance my best for Him. There was always a snag—no music, no space, nothing that is essential for one to perform as an artist.

On this occasion all my pride in work came to the surface and had its first battering from Baba.

It was rather like being a goat. From crag to crag I leapt, accompanying the leaps by a few flappy arm movements. No meaning at all. It could not have been worse, and it certainly did not help when Kenneth Ross produced his bagpipes and started them off, whining and wheezing!

It must have seemed to some of the people there that this strange woman was slightly unbalanced.

I wondered myself.

One Never Won

Long ago in the early days with Baba, I suppose to make it easier for us to be natural with Him, He said to us, "Since you cannot come to my level, I have to come to yours." All the same, however daring one became, one never got the better of Him in fun and wit.

A small group of us were travelling with Him by train to Southampton from where He was sailing to India. On the train journey, He called me over to sit by Him and He then proceeded to explain to me on His alphabet board the difference between Purusha and Prakriti. It was very remiss of me, but my mind was not fully on what He was telling me.

My eyes kept creeping up to His face, instead of completely focussing on what He was telling me. His face was so full of loving beauty that my lack of concentration can easily be understood, and perhaps excused. When He had finished He sat back and said, "Now repeat what I have been telling you." Much abashed, I made a stupendous effort and managed to stumble through the explanation that He had just given me.

It was such a relief to me that I had managed this that I said gaily, "Now you are my first disciple," and quick as lightning He came back with, "And the last."

One never won.

Another story about not winning also started in a train.

In 1931, several persons were travelling with Baba from Devonshire to London, and I was fortunate enough to be sitting on His right side. Suddenly a look of intense interest came over His face and He looked past me and out of the window. Naturally, I turned to see what was interesting Him so much. There was absolutely nothing of any particular interest, some grass, some trees, but nothing else, and as I turned back to Baba, He lightly smacked the side of my face.

Now this trick went on for quite a long time, and I was always caught.

After some months He dropped it, but strange to relate, years later He again revived it, and I was just as dumb as before. He always caught me.

In 1956 while we were in San Francisco with a large group of people who loved Him and who had come to be with Him, He called me and all the dancers who loved Him to go and sit with Him without the rest of the party. It was a high point moment. He gave us no spiritual talk but sat quietly and lovingly with us. Moments of stillness with Him were always my favorites. So warm and so charged with love.

I was sitting at his feet and suddenly He pointed to the back of the room. I turned, thinking He meant to indicate some special dancer, but saw nothing particularly of interest, turned my head back to Him and, lo and behold, He gave my face the same kind of smack that it had not had since the early days with Him. We sat on with Him for some little time longer, when suddenly He again pointed, apparently at someone at the other end of the room. I thought that at last my turn to win had come and I said, "Oh no, Baba, not again. You will not be able to catch me again like that for 700 years." Referring, of course, to His next incarnation. He sighed, looked sad and made out that He was disappointed.

Some three hours later, He sent for me. He stood in the doorway of His room with a worried look on His face and started at once to make signs about something He wished me to do. I stood facing Him, trying to make out what He was telling me. Suddenly He looked up over my left shoulder, and a look of loving welcome dawned on His face. I, of course, wondering who was looking over my shoulder, turned my head, saw no one there, and on turning my face back to Baba received a good hard smack. As I say, one could not win. Strangely enough, that was the last time He ever did this to me.

Paris and Marseilles

N ear the end of 1931, Baba sent for His group of English disciples to meet Him in Paris. It was a strange time for beginners such as we were. For one thing, Meredith was again trying to show us that he was a kind of intermediary through whom we should go to Baba. In fact, although he did not actually say so, he tried to convey to us that his orders were as valid as those that Baba would give us. This did not please Baba, who wanted to train us to be supple to His wishes and orders, and it ended by Meredith and his wife Margaret being sent back to England.

After their departure, Baba's talks to us became clearer. Before that, Meredith had caused a certain mental confusion by explaining to us from his point of view what Baba had really meant. At this time Baba gave me a strict order not to go to East Challacombe when He was not in the West.

We did the usual sightseeing in Paris, the Louvre and such. And on a piercingly cold day, we went to the top of the Eiffel Tower.

Every day from a nearby florist, three white flowers from Quentin Tod, who was in London, would be delivered at the hotel for Baba. Quentin sent an explanation that they signified, "I love you."

From Paris, Baba was going to Marseilles, en route for India, and one morning He announced that since my French was so good, I should escort Him from Paris to the boat, while the others should return to England.

There was a sudden silence. Everyone knew that my French, although passably fluent, had an unmistakable English accent. No one, however, came out with what they thought. They were kind, and I, hypocritically, also remained silent.

On the train, I slept in the compartment next to Baba and His Indian men disciples. He told me that if He knocked on the wall three times it meant, "I love you," and I was to reply in the same manner. This He did several times during the night, and since as far as possible I did not wish to miss out on any of these communications, I hardly slept. Marseilles in the morning seemed rather a blurred spot.

We took the luggage straight to the liner and then went to a restaurant on the quay for breakfast.

Meredith had solemnly told us that Baba would not tolerate facial make-up and sundry other things of the same type, thus even causing Delia to get rid of some valuable furs. While having breakfast, Baba kept looking at me. Finally, with a delicate movement, He drew together his fingers and thumb tips and gently patted his cheeks. I turned to Chanji for a translation. Chanji looked puzzled. Baba then did it again. Meredith's warning came back and I thought, "He cannot possibly mean me to powder my face." I did, however, say questioningly, "Powder?" He shook His head, smiling at me encouragingly. I then said unbelievingly, "You don't mean rouge?" Baba looked happy, smiled and nodded, and I went to the ladies' room to improve my dilapidated appearance.

Baba certainly had a wonderful way of clearing away conventional ideas as to how a disciple should appear. He did not encourage the eccentricities sometimes used to express a false spirituality.

After breakfast we took an elevator up to the famous church of The Lady of the Sea, which was situated on the top of a high cliff. On the way to the church, I gave a beggar a small coin. Baba then explained to me that with the coin one also gave some personal sanskaras and this was not really a kind thing to do. So now if I give something to a beggar I say, "This is a present from Baba." It does seem to settle the sanskara problem.

In the church was a well-known and beautiful picture depicting Christ after having been taken down from the cross. Baba read my mind and signalled to Chanji to reassure me that this would not happen to Him in His present incarnation.

Late in the afternoon Baba, wanting I think to get rid of me, took me to the station and saw me onto the first train to Paris, saying that if I waited until His boat departed it would not be safe for me to be alone in a city like Marseilles. It was probably the largest center of white slave traffic in Europe—but I was 39 years old!

Disobedience—Meredith

After His first visit to England in 1931, Baba on His way to America visited Constantinople. He then went on to Genoa, from where He sailed to New York.

Meredith Starr accompanied Baba and the Indian disciples on this trip. He was at that time trying so hard —in spite of his love for Baba—to prove his importance and independence that he forgot Baba's first wish for everyone was that they should give Him scrupulous obedience.

Early one morning the train was held up at some very large station, and Meredith on waking decided to go to the nearest washroom and clean up prior to dressing himself. As he passed Baba's compartment, Baba saw him and signed to him not to go to the washroom at this time. Seeing no reason for this order, Meredith decided to go anyway.

He had on a knee-length dressing gown, his legs were bare, and he carried his sponge bag and a small towel. The washroom was in the next carriage, behind the one in which his berth was situated. When Meredith had finished his ablutions, he started back towards his berth, but found that in the meantime some shunting and uncoupling had taken place, and that Baba and the rest of the train had disappeared!

And all because of a small piece of disobedience, poor Meredith, a very pompous gentleman, had to wander half-clad round a large international station, causing a certain amount of amusement as he searched for the runaway train. And he had no sense of humor to help ease the situation for him!

One Who Left Baba

One man disciple, who loved Baba deeply, after a year or two left Him. He had been unable to change his predetermined attitude about what was right and what was wrong, and even tried to apply to Baba some rather straightlaced standards. I imagine that up to the time of meeting Baba his highest ideal might have been a bishop.

He was a young man who had given up a great deal for other persons and had lived his life as far as possible in a true Christian spirit, so much so that it had caused a certain spiritual rigidity.

In the summer of 1932, Baba met His close English disciples in Santa Margherita, where everything for us was like an enchanted dream. Sitting on the sands with Baba, wandering over the wooded hills with Him, plus the crystal beauty of the blue Mediterranean—it was like a dream, filled with the sweetness of Baba.

One afternoon we took a walk along the Coastal Road as far as Rapallo. To our surprise, Baba, who was never extravagant, stopped in front of a most elegant tea shop and indicated that the party should go in and drink tea. He supplied a further surprise by ordering a most lavish meal: tea, coffee, iced tea, iced coffee, ice cream cakes, etc., and although we had eaten a good Italian spaghetti-type luncheon, everyone joined in the fun with Baba. Except this one disciple. His face grew longer, and he became withdrawn and unhappy looking.

You may remember the Biblical incident when Mary of Bethany, out of her love for Jesus, anointed His feet with a valuable spice and ointment. When reprimanded by Judas to the effect that the money should have gone to the poor, Christ in answer said, "The poor ye have always with you, but me ye have not always with you." It may not seem possible, but 2000 years later the same incident repeated itself in a slightly different way. Unable to hold his disapproval in check any longer, Baba's disciple leaned forward over the table and said, "Baba, there are poor in the world." Baba smiled but spelt out no verbal reply. He answered, however, by handing the bill to this disciple to pay!

A few days later, we went down on the beach and were strolling happily along when Baba brought another matter to a head for this same disciple.

There was on the beach a most elegant tent. It looked as if it were made of real satin but was, of course, nothing of the kind. Baba looked at it, turned to face us, indicating its charm, then went towards it, opened the flap and peered inside. It contained cushions and a certain number of beach chairs, a most comfortable place to sit and rest. Baba then opened the flap more fully, went inside and called us to go in and sit down—which we did, all except this rigid disciple, who looked shocked and said accusingly, "No English gentleman would do this."

He then turned and left the tent and went to sit on a rock by the sea. A short time after this, the owners of the tent put in an appearance. They behaved beautifully. I think Baba must have thrown out a special wave of love, because they treated the group as welcome guests and said that we could use the tent at any time. I do not think that "the English gentlemen" was pleased about this reception. It seemed as if he felt that those charming persons should have reprimanded us, instead of behaving with such graciousness.

A year or two later, finding that he could neither accept Baba's simplicity and freedom nor give up his own ideas of right and wrong, he left Baba and up to the present time has not returned.

The First Journey to India

At first Baba, in order to bend our wills to His will without His Love being too strong for us, came every few months to be with us in Europe, but not for long periods. The heightening of the Love within and the consequent growth in us of our wish to do whatever He wanted (but in our own way) was exhausting. Even after a few days with Him, we felt drained.

The first year He came several times. To East Challacombe, to London, to Paris, to East Challacombe, to Lugano, to Portofino, and to a hotel in Kensington. In that order. He then stopped coming, and instead sent a message that in the spring of 1933 He wished us to break our Western ties and come to live in India with Him.

There naturally were difficulties for all of us. Families for some people, money for others; in fact it was not easy for anyone. We were all shaken out of our nice grooves.

At that time I had a flourishing school of ballet, was teaching for the Sadler's Wells Ballet Company (afterwards the Royal Ballet), was choreographer to the Carl Rosa Opera, and so on. The only way to go to Baba was to break all contracts and sell the school. As soon as the news of my unexplainable behavior got around the dancing world, my telephone rang from morning to night, bringing me attacks from friends and enemies about my foolishness. Remember, this was before

World War II, before the days when teenagers could say "goodbye" to their families, stagger away with a pack on the back, and set out for India, Nepal and other spots in search of gurus, yogis, masters. We were possibly the first group of ordinary persons to embark on a trip of this kind.

The English contingent crossed the Channel, went to Paris, where we met Elizabeth, Norina and Vivienne, took the train to Genoa, and then embarked on the S.S. Victoria en route for India.

Our party aroused a great deal of curiosity on the boat. It was the hot season in India and quite the wrong time for tourists to be going to the East. Tea planters, army officers and their wives, and businessmen were understandable, but tourists? No. Curiosity made our fellow travelers ask quite impertinent questions; and since we had agreed not to tell anyone what we were really going to do in India, we stuck to the tourist picture.

One of our party, softened by sitting in the moonlight, told our story to some young man. This, later on, had quite serious consequences.

We also suffered from Vivienne. She was a protégé of Norina's who had persuaded Baba to allow her to come, on the grounds that she was of a much higher spiritual quality than any of the English group. She was a dancer of the Isadora Duncan school of thought, and told us more times than even our politeness thought was necessary that on the night of Isadora's death she had heard a voice (Isadora's, I presume) say, "My mantle has fallen on Vivienne." She would sit on deck in the moonlight, her gramophone pouring out Chopin, her head poised at exactly the same angle as Isadora's in some of her photographs, gazing ecstatically at the moon. Norina, looking at her admiringly, would say to us, "She is so spiritual." The rest of us were bored.

One evening someone, irritated with this continual comparing of Vivienne's spiritual qualities with our apparent lack of them, said, "Why do you always say spiritual? That Chopin music is purely romantic!" We did not hear so much after that of our rival's superior spirituality.

We were met at Bombay by many of Baba's disciples and devotees who draped garlands of flowers round our necks and treated us as very special persons. We stayed for a day or two at the Majestic Hotel, without seeing Baba, and were taken round to see the sights of Bombay. We were then taken to a pleasant house not far from Bombay. Baba was staying there with Mehera, Mani and several other women who constituted Baba's Eastern women mandali. These were the women with whom afterwards we were to spend a long period of ashram life.

It was wonderful to be once more with Baba, to see His loving eyes light with pleasure at our arrival. All the difficulties of getting to Him seemed in one moment to be wiped away.

Before leaving for Kashmir, Baba insisted that our passports should receive visas to enable us to go to China, and that we should have everything ready to go to America, where He would break His silence in the Hollywood Bowl, at which moment we should receive God-realization. The latter trip had been spoken of before we started on this trip, and Minta and Norina, being both actresses and beautiful women, saw a picture in their mind's eyes and bought beautiful and expensive dresses to look well for the occasion.

The journey as far as Rawalpindi was made by train, and on the way we stayed at Agra for a short time, and from there we went to spend an evening at the Taj Mahal. Somehow Baba had arranged that our visit to this unbelievably beautiful place should coincide with the rising of the full moon at the back of the Taj, leaving us spellbound at the entrance gate. Baba's Love, the beauty of the Taj, the slowly rising moon and the dark blue of the Indian sky met together in an enchantment never to be forgotten or repeated. After a spellbound and silent interval, we walked forward with Baba along paths which ran beside dark water and led to the building itself. We spent some time admiring the workmanship, and once more went over the romantic story of Shah Jehan and his creation of so much beauty in memory of his beloved Mumtaz.

Vivienne, who, whenever asked, had refused to dance for Baba with a plea that the floor was all wrong or there was no room or the artistic atmosphere was not inspiring, decided that the Taj was the place that completely filled her requirements. She said this loudly. Baba did not invite her to dance.

We went to the Taj again the next morning and, although the beauty in the morning sunlight was there as before, somehow one missed the moon magic.

This was the high point of the trip, and that very day events began to turn in an unexpected and unpleasing direction.

Baba told a few of us that His arrangements were not going according to plan and that if matters did not straighten out with the government, He might have to send us back to Europe, where we should wait until He joined us. It all sounded most nebulous and, though there was an uncomfortable feeling, I think we also had a feeling that everything would be all right.

We then continued the journey to Srinagar. There Baba had arranged for us to stay on houseboats and from there trips—mostly in smallboats—were taken to see the beautiful Kashmir country. One day Baba took the party to Harvan, a place with an open view stretching across flat country to a not-too-far-away range of mountains. He pointed out a part of the mountain and told us that this was the spot to which the body of Jesus had been brought and buried. We were very moved.

Norina and Minta were so overcome by the inherent drama of the moment that they hurriedly picked grasses and flowers and flung themselves at Baba's feet. Baba looked at them, made no sign, and then spelt out, "And now we will go and see the Maharajah's trout!"

We went to many beauty spots, including the famous Shalimar Gardens, and although all this was most enjoyable, the feeling that we were going to be sent back grew stronger and stronger until Baba sadly announced that, as He had feared, circumstances made it impossible to continue with His original plans. We must go to Europe and wait for Him there. A shattered and not very happy group was motored to Rawalpindi, put on a train that went straight through to Bombay, and directly to the docks. There we embarked on a Scottish liner, parted from Baba, and the next day steamed out to sea.

Our spirits went lower and lower, and I would suggest that no one should ever travel in the tropics on a Scottish liner. This one was pervaded by a peculiar smell and by porridge and other Scottish delicacies that did not help our recovery.

We had, however, not completely reached the bottom of the barrel. That was yet to come. The young man to whom Minta on the outward journey had confided our real purpose in going to India had some connection with the press and had cabled this story to England. The newspapers, having a slack season, jumped at the story and turned it into goodness knows what. Journalists called on our friends, and Delia's brothers, who did not approve of Baba, handed out plenty of information. And now we were coming back! Cables, with prepayment for answers, reached us, asking why this was so. Were we disillusioned? Answers were sent out to the effect that we were returning to prepare the way for Meher Baba to come to the West.

As the boat neared Marseilles, where supposedly we were to disembark and wait in the neighborhood for Baba to join us, a cable from India brought us instructions to go on to England where Baba would join us. The docks at Marseilles were crowded with journalists. The European papers also thought they were onto a good thing and had sent representatives. "Why had we returned?" I am sure they were hoping for some scandalous story and were disappointed at the "preparing the way for Meher Baba" statement, the only thing that any of us would say.

The boat went on to Liverpool, and we remained on board. Here again, we were met by press representatives, and again there were more at Paddington station. These had managed to squeeze out some columns and even obtain some photos from our friends. The surprising thing is that at that time none of the papers said or insinuated anything unpleasant about Baba.

We hung about London for some weeks, and then were summoned to meet Baba in Portofino.

The Queen, the Cardinal, and the Grand Duchess

I t was understandable that Norina, because of the ordinary middle-class positions of most of Baba's close disciples, did not feel that they could possibly be of any use to Baba, and she told them so.

In her mind, the best way to publicize Baba's work would be for Baba to be in a situation somewhat like that of Rasputin and the Czarina. So out of her great love for Him she pulled social strings, resulting at last in a cable received in Portofino from the Queen of Roumania, one of the few royalties at that time left with a country.

The cable said: "The Queen of Roumania is prepared to receive Meher Baba." Baba replied: "Meher Baba is prepared to receive the Queen of Roumania."

Soon after this, Baba left Portofino to spend a few days in Rome, where Norina's husband had held an important diplomatic position and where it was easy for her to bring important persons to meet Baba. The most important, a well-known Cardinal, was one hour late for his appointment. Baba refused to see him.

Some years later, in India, a Russian Grand Duchess came to meet Baba and stay in the ashram. The visit was not a success. When this unprepared lady found that she had to sleep on the floor on a bedding roll, share a bathroom with several other people, and experience other discomforts, she after a short time departed to the more congenial home of a Maharajah friend.

Years later, just before she died, Norina told me that the people she loved most and had come to really care for were Baba's ordinary disciples and that she had no more interest in royalty as a means of spreading the love of Baba.

Through his love, Baba had marvelously wiped Norina free from this sanskara. Along the way, he had seemingly wiped Europe free from most of its royal families as well.

Theatrical Things

Many of Baba's early disciples were in some way or other connected with the theatre. Delia, with her brother, ran a tryout theatre in Kew. Quentin Tod directed the Midnight Follies and did a great deal of work for Andre Chalot, the famous producer. I was a dancer and choreographer, Minta was an actress.

To use all that we had in His service, Baba would demand a performance, sometimes giving adequate time to do a good job and sometimes only enough time to give some not-so-good improvisations. And since we were still in the stage where we were accepting His statement, "I have come to your level," we enjoyed making small skits about things going on in His work with us at that time.

In Portofino we wrote a skit. In it, we had all become old and tottery—quite a wonderful piece of foresight—and were sitting around for Baba's next announcement about His speaking. After some idiotic conversation, the door opened and in came a jaunty Quentin. He was dressed in shorts and had an Alpine hat with a fluttery feather standing straight up at the back.

We stared myopically and then turned to each other, speculating on whether at last this was "the Perfect Boy." For some time, Baba had been sending some of His disciples to search for the Perfect Boy, who was in some way necessary for His work. At the time of the play, he had not yet appeared, although various imperfect boys had been brought for Baba's inspection, including one who was cross-eyed and another rather bowlegged creature, causing some caustic comments on Western ideas of perfection.

After Quentin's entry someone asked, "Do you speak English?"

The boy proudly said, "Yes, yes."

Several other languages were tried, and he passed with flying colors. "Da, da. Si, si. Oui, oui."

We old ladies were deeply impressed and nodded our elderly heads, signifying "at last."

A knock on the door and in came Kaka in a mailman's get-up, bringing a cable from Baba. Delia, with trembling old fingers, managed to open it and in a cracked old voice read out: "Owing to the eruption of Vesuvius, I shall not speak until April 1st."

All the old ladies either fainted or slipped to the floor, except Delia, who stood up, flung her arms above her head, raised her eyes to heaven, and in a Lady Macbeth kind of voice proclaimed, "I still believe."

Baba laughed. Most viewers seemed to enjoy it, except one Indian disciple who was slightly shocked.

The best show during this early period was given at the Kew Theatre. Jack de Leon helped with the direction, lent his lighting experts, and generally made it possible to put on a variety show in a professional manner. There was a short play, some dancing, a musical comedy number, and other items making about an hour and a half of performances.

There had also been plenty of time for rehearsal while waiting in London for a promised visit from

Baba, and for once all went well.

In India, during the war period, Baba, several times before going off on a mast tour, would ask that we should get a show ready before His return. And however they turned out, with our limited resources, if Baba recognized that we had put our all into it, He would congratulate and embrace us. Those were wonderful times—having nothing and yet making something for Baba.

Second Dance Adventure

I n the spring of 1932 Baba again came to England, bringing with Him Ghani, Nilu, and one or two others of the Indian men's group.

After staying for a short time, He told us that He was going to Lugano for a few days, and wished Kim, Kitty, Delia, Minta and me to accompany Him.

It was lovely to be with Baba by this beautiful lake. But He also gave us some experiences of the ways He worked to bring His disciples to some kind of obedience of even unpleasant orders. The one I am writing about here was another attack on my dancing, much worse than the first.

One wet morning, cars were hired and we went for a drive up into the hills surrounding Lugano. The rain steadily got worse and we could see nothing, so we halted at a small Swiss village and went into the local coffee shop. The place was full of locals having a mid-morning cup of coffee.

We all sat down, and Baba suddenly spotted, near to where we were sitting, a rather broken-down gramophone and a quantity of equally broken-down records. He made signs of pleasure and told Ghani to put on a record, and then signed that I should dance. I was unprepared for this fresh assault on my dancing. I did my best to improvise to some impossible piece of music which flowed out from a cracked record.

Again heavy boots and country clothes, and the

only thing I could do was to hop about and run in and out among the tables.

The locals stopped their conversations and undisguisedly stared at me. Some then started to whisper knowingly, nodding their heads in my direction.

I was thankful when the record ended its raucous noise, and I was moving over to my seat when Baba made a sign to Ghani to turn over the record and motioned to me to continue.

He signified that He was enjoying this dreadful performance. For about twenty minutes this went on. From record to record. Then Baba stopped the whole affair and I slunk miserably to my seat.

The cafe settled down to its usual morning activities while Baba looked radiant and as if nothing untoward had happened.

Alice Traw Fischer

I n the summer of 1933 after our first trip to India, we stayed with Baba in a charming Italian house in Portofino.

It overlooked the blue Mediterranean, and the grounds ran for some distance along the top of a rocky cliff, which dropped down to the sea. Here we often walked with Baba in beauty and joy.

Visiting Baba at this time was Alice Traw Fischer, the principal soprano from one of the German opera houses.

She looked like a singer. Raised rib cage, good carriage, carefully fitted dresses. She could have walked onto a stage at any given moment, but more important than all this, she loved Baba deeply.

During the cliff walks, Baba would stop and make signs to Alice that He would like her to sing. With no fuss, such as being unable to find the right pitch without an accompanist, or that she should have a preliminary warming up of the throat, she would stand still and her beautiful voice, with no apparent effort, would float out along the cliff top, giving Baba pleasure both with her singing and her immediate obedience.

Years later, at the beginning of World War II, she and her husband were in such difficulties that they decided to try to get away from Europe and go to America. They were allowed to take very few possessions with them. A few clothes and a small amount of money.

They decided, however, to take a big risk, and some jewels were hidden in the bottom of a trunk.

The customs officer meticulously examined and shook out each garment, pinched anything that looked suspicious, gradually but surely coming down to the hidden treasures. Alice told me that she stood there full of fear, not asking Baba for anything, rather simply concentrating on His Love.

Suddenly, just as hope had almost gone, another customs officer rushed into the room saying that he had found someone trying to smuggle something important out of the country, and that the other officer must come at once. He hurriedly pushed Alice's clothes back in the trunk and rushed away to attend to the other matter.

After the war, I met Alice and her husband in San Francisco. They were very poor. She was giving music lessons and he was selling imitation jewelry.

Her love for Baba had grown enormously. I believe that after the war she returned to Europe, found her house empty and since her singing days were over, she opened a boarding house. This, however, I have never had confirmed.

The Ghost

I n the summer of 1933, after our return from India, Baba was with us in Portofino, staying in a beautiful house upon a cliff overlooking the Mediterranean.

The house was supposed to be haunted by a spirit who needed to be freed from this world and who apparently hoped that Baba would do this. No one ever saw this ghost, but one disciple said that she awoke to find her hair being violently pulled. Another one heard a loud, sharp bang on the wall beside her.

Some of the bedrooms had French windows that opened onto a terrace overlooking the sea. One night, being unable to sleep, I stepped outside, sat down on a low wall overlooking the "wine-dark sea" and watched some fishing boats with large lanterns moving across the horizon and a few other nocturnal craft flitting about under a star-studded bowl.

I remained for some time immersed in this wonderful place, thinking idly of Baba. Not a deep meditation, but just enjoying this place with Him. On my way back to my room I stopped and peered into the window of a room shared by a few disciples. Unfortunately, Delia was awake, took me for the ghost and started to scream, rousing the others who also started to make an outcry.

Not realizing that I was the cause of the trouble, I leaned farther forward, putting my face right on the window and my arms above my head for balance. The bedroom door opened and some others came in to inquire into the cause of the noise. Baba sent Kaka over from the other side of the house and I was shooed away from the window. No one seemed pleased with me.

The next morning we were sitting happily around the breakfast table, with the sunlight flitting along the floor and all the night's woes forgotten, when Baba, full of light and energy, strode in and sat down on the edge of an unused table. He looked round at us and appeared to be smiling at His own thoughts. He then called someone to read and spelled out on the board: "There is one thing that I admire about my Western disciples."

At this point I think that everyone preened themselves a little. Admiration! Well . . . ! Baba looked around and then went on: "It is their courage."

The preening stopped hurriedly. Baba then took pity on us and got us all laughing with Him at ourselves.

The Dark Night

One summer in the early 1930's Baba did not come to the West, so Delia, Quentin, Mabel and I went for a short holiday to Portofino, a place that held for us so many loving memories of being there with Baba. One early sunlit morning, Delia and I were having an early breakfast outside a small restaurant in the square, when for some unknown reason we started up an argument about the dark night of the soul, about which neither of us knew a great deal. As usual in such cases, the argument became quite heated. Suddenly a most delightful-looking woman appeared at our table, laughing and saying, "Do you mind if I join you? I have never heard anyone argue about the dark night of the soul at breakfast!" Well, the upshot of this was that she joined our small group at swimming and at walking over the hills and, of course, she heard a great deal about Baba. We did consign the dark night to its proper place.

This woman, whose name I have completely forgotten, turned out to be a member of one of the famous English shipping families, and she was writing a book about her impressions of this Italian holiday. We parted at the end of the summer, having enjoyed the short friendship.

Some years later, in 1946 after my return from India, this woman came up to me in Piccadilly Circus.

After exchanging greetings, she said that she was sure I would be interested in what she was going to tell me.

Apparently, shortly after her Italian holiday, she was at a dinner party and to make some amusing small talk, she brought out the story of the strange people she had met in Portofino and of their devotion to and belief in Meher Baba. To her surprise, a Cabinet Minister who was present seemed to know about Baba. He said that owing to some complaints made about Baba to Scotland Yard (by Meredith Starr and another disciple who had left Baba and wanted to be nasty) searching inquiries had been made, but that nothing whatsoever had been found against Baba, and in fact the reports about His work had been excellent.

After at least ten years and a war between this and our last meeting, to take the trouble to assure me that Baba stood well with the government was an amazing piece of thoughtfulness. I feel that it did bring her a little closer to Him. I hope so.

The Looking Glass

During the early days of Baba's visits to England, a young and extremely competent dancer, who was a very matter-of-fact, down-to-earth type, was fortunate enough to meet Baba and to dance for Him. Afterwards she did not discuss with me what she had felt about Him, and I therefore concluded that the meeting with Baba had not meant much to her.

One day about a year later she came to me in a puzzled state of mind, saying that she had had a strange experience.

She said that she had a bedroom which had length but not a great deal of width. It had at one end a looking glass which almost covered the wall and at the opposite end was the door. One afternoon she entered the room and was taken aback to see Baba standing inside the looking glass with His hand stretched out towards her and on His face a loving smile. She felt strongly the wonder and beauty of this, but had no idea what she should do. She stood still, and then began to walk towards Him. She suddenly thought, "If I can see Him in the looking glass, He must be standing just behind me," and she turned away from the looking glass to look back towards the door. This was a mistake, for when she did not see Him she again turned to the looking glass, and Baba was no longer there.

One sometimes wonders about stories of this kind, but since this girl was a straightforward type, it seems acceptable.

Many years later, after the war, Baba went to London and many people went to the Charing Cross Hotel to renew earlier contacts or to meet Him for the first time and to feel at close quarters the Love that at all times flowed from Him.

This girl had, by this time, become in the dance field a most successful young woman. When she heard that Baba was giving interviews, she felt a strong urge to go to Him.

This time it was very different from the first meeting. She afterwards wrote to me that she could now feel the warmth and beauty of His love and that her own love for Him was strong and sure.

The Chart

Baba, with a group of Eastern and Western disciples plus a few other persons who were beginning to love Baba, went for a short time to stay with Hedi and Walter Mertens at their home near Zurich. Among the visitors was the famous film director Gabriel Pascal, who was, according to hearsay, the only person that Bernard Shaw would allow to direct the film versions of his plays. When Pascal was in his great-director moods, he was inclined to be pompous and important, but at other times he could be full of fun and as simple as a child. Especially when he was near Baba.

He would sit on the floor at Baba's feet, looking like an entranced child, and listen avidly to any talks that Baba might be giving.

One day Baba produced an enormous chart, which illustrated the evolution of man, and had it hung beside Him on the wall. Then, aided by someone with a long stick who pointed out various things on the chart, He gave an interesting talk on the physical evolution of man, and at the same time made comments on his spiritual evolution.

When Baba came to the climax of the lecture, He announced that the missing link theory was a mistaken one, and that He himself would tell us the truth about the matter. Pascal was absolutely ecstatic. Baba looked extremely solemn and said that the next day He would finish this talk. But the next day, no talk.

And Baba's explanation has simply joined the link.

Quentin

Quentin Tod, an early Western disciple, toured America with Baba and accompanied Him to many other places.

Quentin was a charmer. Quentin in white tie and tails was a more than acceptable escort. He worked successfully in the theatre directing sections of revues for Andre Chalot and he also directed the Midnight Follies.

He met Baba in 1931, immediately felt Baba's love and started to work for Him, introducing to Him many theatrical celebrities. For instance, the actor and director Ivor Novello invited Baba to a revue which was running successfully in London. At the end of the performance the whole cast aknowledged their applause by bowing to Baba, who was sitting in the stage box. Quentin traveled with Baba in America and was instrumental in bringing into contact with Him many movie stars, including Mary Pickford (who I believe asked to meditate with Him), Tallulah Bankhead, and others.

In 1937 Baba and His close disciples went to stay just outside Zurich at the spacious home of Walter Mertens. Here it was that the following incident occurred.

Walter asked Baba if He would serve His disciples some wine made from special grapes grown on the estate. Usually we had no wine but Baba agreed to serve this special wine. Everyone was happy about this. We knew it would mean taking the Sacrament with

Our Lord, and that it should be a rare and beautiful occasion.

Now somehow a German woman, not really loving Baba, had managed to plant herself in the house, and in a curious way was rejected by Baba. It was not a direct rejection such as asking her to leave, but nevertheless it was there.

Baba sent for Quentin and told him to tell this woman as tactfully as possible not to come to the evening gathering. It is important to understand that if someone should receive an order personally the task should be fulfilled by the person to whom the work was given, and not handed on to anyone else.

Therefore, when Quentin, not even explaining the matter to her fully, asked Enid Corfe to give Baba's message to the woman, an unpleasant situation arose.

Enid apparently failed to realize how important it was to make this woman understand that she must not come to the gathering. She completely forgot to tell her.

In the evening about 20 of us went happily to join Baba and to share in the festivity. He looked radiant and happy, and the whole room was redolent with His love, warm and deep. And the evening promised to be an outstanding time of joy.

He started to pour about half an inch of wine into the glasses, and handed them one at a time to each of us. We were prepared to drink the Wine of Love with Baba.

Alas! Just as everything seemed to be washed over with peace and beauty, the door opened and in came the German woman.

For a moment Baba looked at her—and then turned a reproachful look on Quentin, who went red in the face, almost burst into tears and began wild and meaningless apologies.

Then beautifully and gently Baba, as a sign of forgiveness, held out a glass of wine to him. Quentin was, however, so overwrought and upset that he could not bring himself to accept this token of Baba's loving forgiveness. He said, "Oh no, Baba, I could not take it." Three times Baba offered the wine and three times Quentin refused it. Baba's mood then changed to a kind of sternness, and He sent the rest of us away, disappointed and uncertain, while He kept Quentin with Him.

What transpired between Him and Quentin we never heard, but it was from this time on that Quentin gradually seemed to change and to drift slowly away from Baba.

Second Quentin Story

I n spite of Quentin's great love for Baba, and there was no mistake about that, he again, through a lack of understanding that obedience should be immediate and self eliminating, failed to respond to Baba's wishes.

Prior to sailing for Bombay, Baba was staying at a hotel in Marseilles. He was accompanied by a small group of Eastern and Western disciples. Someone—I do not remember who—had given Baba an enormous birdcage. There were no birds in this contraption. Therefore, during the wait for the ship, Baba would send disciples out to buy and bring to the hotel small cages of budgerigars, which were then transferred to the big bird cage. Since in London Quentin had owned quite a large collection of these birds, he was given the job of transferring the birds from the small cages into the large one.

Now Quentin, even though an American by birth, had while living in England acquired the habit of having a cup of tea during the afternoon and he traveled with a small spirit stove so that this ceremony should not be missed.

He had on one occasion just got everything well on the way. The water was on the point of boiling when someone arrived, triumphantly carrying another cage of the small birds.

Baba happily signalled to Quentin to do his job, but

was met by, "Oh, wait a minute, Baba, the water is just coming to the boil."

Baba immediately gave a sign to someone else to see to the transfer.

It was a disaster. The disciple who received the order did his best but he was not used to birds and they escaped from his inexperienced hands and fluttered away.

Again Quentin was overcome by his mistake, but from this time on, little by little, he drew away from Baba, and after some months, not long before World War II, he broke away from Baba altogether. During the war he had no communication with Him at all.

There is, however, a brighter ending to this story. After the war, which I had spent in India with Baba, I returned to England for a short time and there Quentin got in touch with me. We spent a wonderful afternoon in Kew Gardens, talking lovingly of Baba, and he told me that his love for Baba had returned and was much stronger than before the break. A short time after my arrival in America, I heard that Quentin had died. His death had been caused by war-time malnutrition.

Dancing With God

During the summer of 1932 Baba came to Santa Margherita, Italy, to be with a group of His English disciples.

We stayed in a small hotel overlooking the Mediterranean and spent lovely days walking over the nearby hills with Baba, or sitting on the sands and perhaps listening to a short discourse or perhaps sitting quietly watching the wash of small, crystal blue waves, and experiencing a released happiness. Occasionally there was an expedition to the hills or a nearby town.

One trip to the hills at Portofino Vetta was quite different from anything else we usually did with Baba. A kind of "wagonette" was hired for the trip. We picked masses of wild flowers and decorated it, decorated the horses (two), decorated ourselves, and Baba allowed us to put a garland round His neck. We all got in and the wagonette started off for the hills.

As we passed through Santa Margherita, Baba's beauty and the gaiety of the group round Him attracted a great deal of interest. Several persons waved and smiled in greeting and Baba positively shone with love. The Italian temperament seemed to blend in with and enjoy our passing by.

On arriving at a valley in the hills, we had a picnic luncheon and afterwards a short rest. We then walked with Baba under the trees and through the valley, and at times sat round Him on the short grass. Nothing was planned; it all happened as Baba indicated at the moment.

The day, however, ended a little sadly. An Englishwoman who had arrived the day before, unexpectedly and uninvited by Baba, was told by Him that she could not remain. This threw a damper on the return trip. Baba explained that this time had been allotted to finding and beginning to train His close Western disciples, and when this had been completed and the training was on its way, then others who loved Him would be able to come closer.

One afternoon several persons had to go into the nearby town and have something done to their passports. Delia and I did not go. Our passports were in order. After the midday meal and the departure of the others, we went out into the walled garden at the back of the small hotel and settled down, expecting to have a quiet hour. But no. Something better was in store for us. Suddenly Baba and Chanji appeared and came to join us. This was a treat, to have Him all to ourselves, plus all His attention. We did not regret the absence of our friends.

Baba was in a playful mood. He made signs and Chanji translated that Baba had said that I should give Him a dancing lesson. This was fun of the highest order. Chanji took Baba's hand and brought Him to class. I then took His hand and showed Him a simple 1-2-3 hop step. No obstacles. He took it at once and then, hand in hand, we flew round the garden path. And I really mean flew. He could move as no one else has ever moved—with joy, freedom, rhythm. And I knew, without intellectualizing it, that dancing was, is, and always will be a part of God.

That short holiday in Italy will always stand out in memory. Baba showed us clearly at that time what He meant when He said, "You cannot come to My level, so I have come to yours."

In later years the difference in treatment was enormous. The Love was always there, but Baba dealt with our recalcitrant egos from His level.

The Nasik Period

*I am the Divine Beloved,
worthy of being loved
because I am Love.*

MEHER BABA

Stories from Nasik

In late 1936, Baba summoned a small group of us to India to stay in Nasik for an unspecified period. The English group consisted of Delia, Kitty, Will and Mary Backett and Tom Sharpley. Jean Adriel, Malcolm Schloss, Elizabeth, Norina, Nadine and a few others came from America.

We left London and crossed the channel en route to Marseilles, and on arriving in Paris we heard that Edward VIII had abdicated from the English throne in order to marry Mrs. Simpson. On board ship in Marseilles we heard his abdication speech. We stayed in Nasik for some months, heard the coronation of the new king described over the radio, and the next day Baba put into action the difficulties that caused the Nasik ashram to be broken up and both Americans and English to return for a time to their respective countries.

We arrived in Nasik on Christmas Eve. Baba, accompanied by Kaka, came to dinner at the ashram and made it for us a celebration. After dinner Baba announced that Kaka wished to make a speech. Kaka's English was practically nonexistent, but he waved his arms, was desperately earnest and repeated at intervals the words "no touch," which was about all most of us could grasp of the speech. When he finally sat down, bathed in triumph, we naturally applauded, but were no wiser than when he began. Baba, with an amused look, spelt on the board: "It seems that Kaka disapproves of marriage."

As soon as we were settled in, Baba arranged for Ramjoo to give us lessons in Hindustani.

I think, when faced by this strange collection of Westerners, he slightly lost his head because the first sentence he taught us was, "Mai khudar residah hoon," meaning "I am God-realized." So useful.

This later on had an amusing sequel.

Gary Fort, a Hollywood writer, who among other things had written the script for "Dracula," came to India with Jean Adriel to be with Baba. He had theatrical ideas about strange white monasteries in Tibet and, although I believe he came to love Baba, he was, I think, disappointed in the simplicity of life at Nasik. After a few months he went to Baba and said that it was impossible to write an account of spiritual life in India just by living in Nasik!

Baba then sent him away, with Chanji as guide, to see some other sides of Indian life.

They went to many places, and I believe stayed in some second class Hindu hotels, which invariably seem to have a strange, unpleasant smell. In those days, blue jeans had not appeared on the scene as the accepted uniform for everyone, and Gary was well dressed—white solar topi, white suit, white shoes—and could not possibly have been taken for anything but a well-to-do American.

When he arrived in Benares and went down to the sacred Ganges, he stood out against all those who came to dip in the holy waters hoping to further their spiritual growth.

He was accosted by one of the many beggars who haunt these places. The man followed him, hands outstretched and with voluble demands for money. He was persistent and after a time Gary, losing his head and his temper, yelled at the beggar, using the only sentence he could remember from the Hindustani lessons:

"Mai khudar residah hoon."

This was too much from someone of Gary's well-to-do, worldly appearance. The beggar fell back terrified, flung up his arms and rushed madly away.

It is said that Baba enjoyed this story.

Another Gary story. Baba, who saw everything and knew that Gary was restless and that he felt confined and tied, sent him, accompanied by one of the mandali, for a few days to Bombay. He came back looking more alive and brought with him a small present for the housekeeping. It was a couple of cans of Heinz Baked Beans which he handed over to Norina, who was in charge of the house.

On reading the label and finding that the cans also contained pork, she was indignant and said that pork was not an acceptable food in an ashram.

When Baba came into the room, she pointed this out to Him. He looked most serious and ordered the cans to be opened and had the small scraps of pork carefully picked out and placed on a dish.

He gave the dish to someone to carry, then, accompanied by all of us, solemnly led the way into the garden. A gardener was called and told to dig up a certain rose bush. The pork was placed in the hole, and the rose bush replanted over it. Baba then smiled happily and left His somewhat mystified disciples.

Whether Baba was teaching us not to fuss when everything was in His hands, I don't know. In any case the rose bush died!

Visiting Under Difficulties—1937

Once a week the Western disciples were taken to Meherabad and the women were taken up the hill to be with Mehera, Mani, Khorshed and the other Eastern women. Up to this time the Eastern and Western groups of women had not been brought together, either for work or for training. This was a beginning, and on these visits we gradually began to learn and recognize each other's personalities, and to have a slight early recognition of the differences in the Eastern and Western approach to life. Later on, when the two groups lived and worked together, these initial meetings made reconciling the differences much easier.

These visits took place during the time that Baba had placed Mehera under a very severe discipline. Everything was arranged to keep her mind all the time on Baba. She and those living with her had to write Baba's name many times every day. With the exception of Baba, she never saw a man or heard a man's name.

We were warned severely not to allow a man's name to creep into our conversations with the girls. You can imagine how difficult this was. In ordinary social conversation the names Tom, Jack, etc., creep naturally into conversation. These are simply part of ordinary social life.

In talking with the girls, it was extremely difficult to be natural. Stilted, thought-out remarks about how dusty the roads had been on the drive over, how much hotter it was in India than it was in the West, and a few more things of the same type, and then communication would fade away while one frantically tried to evolve a remark that held no danger.

One afternoon we were sitting in a circle around Baba when suddenly Norina's social skills took over and she started to be charming and natural. It was fatal. Just as all seemed to be going well, she was carried away and to everyone's horror, especially her own, she came out with "and Tom said," followed by a horrified silence in the room, a silence that could be heard.

Baba quietly turned to Mehera, put her head on His shoulder and assured her that it was quite all right, she was with Him and His Love washed out the hearing of the name.

He then turned forgivingly to Norina, who was tremendously upset by the occurrence.

One afternoon Baba called me aside and said accusingly, "I told the girls that you had a sense of humor and would be great fun, but since these visits started you have been practically silent."

His eyes had a twinkle. All I could say was that having to think so carefully before speaking, it was impossible to be natural.

Baba laughed.

After a few visits, however, everyone got used to the situation, and ease and friendship began to flower. Luckily there were no more misadventures.

Backbiting

Over and over again, Baba emphasized His wish that we should not criticize one another, especially with that form of criticism known as "backbiting." Here is an instance in which He did not give a straightforward correction but without a word showed us what we were doing.

Living with us in the ashram in Nasik was a most charming woman by the name of Ruano. She loved Baba and, not having been told by Him that she should not do so, continued as she had done for some years to smoke cigars.

Well, this roused the critical ire of some of the group, those who had decided ideas of what should or should not be done in the ashram of a great spiritual teacher.

Baba said nothing and, seemingly unaware of it, allowed the affair to go on for some little time. He waited until one day while we were sitting around Him, then He produced a large box of cigars and with a loving smile and gesture presented it to Ruano. The gentle correction was perfectly clear, and after that Ruano smoked in peace. And on that particular issue at least, we were released from the sin of "back-biting."

More Dance Troubles

I n Nasik Baba again took it out of me and my dancing.

For some time there had been a movement among some of Baba's disciples to further Baba's work by finding the means to produce a spiritual film.

Many well-known writers had presented scripts, none of which, up to the Nasik period, was found acceptable by Baba. The production was to be carried through by Gabriel Pascal, the famous director. He loved Baba and, since Baba seemed to want it, was most anxious to do this movie for Him.

One day Baba called me and said that I must set to work and arrange a large dance for this movie. There were to be 120 dancers in the ballet, all moving together to express some kind of spiritual awakening, and since there were no dancers at Nasik, I was to work out the patterns on Rano (representing 60 dancers) and Delia (representing 60 other dancers)!

Every morning the sitting room, in which there was a rather broken-down, untuned piano, would be reserved for this work, and Kitty was told that she must accompany the rehearsals on this ghastly piano.

As to the choice of music, the only piece to be found in the ashram was Schubert's Unfinished Symphony, which was totally unsuitable and much too short for such a large production.

So every morning in the intense heat I tried to work

out patterns for 120 dancers on two rather resentful friends who were inclined to blame me for the whole affair. Kitty at the piano, making no pretense of any interest whatsoever, did not help the uncreative atmosphere. Added to this there was Norina, whose room opened off the sitting room, at intervals dashing out to complain about the endless repetitions of the Unfinished Symphony, plus the complaints of the two dancers, and my own complaints when they would forget and turn in the wrong direction, or have no recollection of what had been arranged the morning before. Then Baba would come in, sit down and ask for explanations of what the rest of the 120 dancers were supposedly doing, and either praise the ideas or cut out a whole section as being unsuitable.

It was more than a relief to everyone concerned when after about two weeks Baba said that nothing more need be done to the ballet until the actual time for the filming should arrive. Which it never did. My love for dancing was not quite killed, and after a long convalescence again became, and remains, vital.

The Backetts

There was a very dear, earnest, married couple staying with the Nasik group.

Their search for God had been a long one, and they had followed certain paths that they considered helpful to them. For instance, their marriage was a celibate one and they carefully avoided eating certain kinds of food; while Mary, the wife, spent much time in weaving a kind of blue material out of which she made her dresses, which had a definite resemblance to the Indian sari. Before going to India someone sent her a length of blue Liberty silk to make one of these garments for the trip. She returned it to the donor, saying that although the material was blue, it was flecked with dark red triangles which, being the color of blood, she could not wear. And they were most distressed that their cabin on the ship in which we travelled to India had no spiritual atmosphere.

After six months in India there was a decided change. Mary had acquired some saris with which to create her robes and having seen Baba himself wear coats of any color, she had simply lost this inhibition and, red included, had bought materials for a very bright wardrobe.

Will, the husband, again complained on the return journey about their cabin, but this time it was noisy and too near the engine. These were two dear, loving persons who had never been annoying with their rigid ideas, and six months with Baba gently melted away a great deal of spiritually inhibiting nonsense.

Holy Man

One day a wandering holy man came to the ashram asking to see Baba. Baba received him with love and lent him a small hut on the grounds in which he might stay and meditate for a few days.

We had with us a slightly competitive lady who was determined to go quickly along the spiritual path. Hearing about the advanced status of this man, she decided to try and get a push from him. She went to the hut, sat beside him on the ground and put her head on his shoulder.

A few minutes later Baba—who certainly knew everything that we were likely to do—came along, opened the flap and beckoned to her to come outside. In no uncertain terms He gave her to understand that someone who had Baba for her master was foolish to go off down a side road, leaving the direct way to Baba. Her action was a hindrance rather than a help.

After He had in no uncertain terms shown her where she had been foolish, He healed the wound with loving words and an embrace. She went away chastened, but wiser and full of love for Baba.

Dreams

A few of the disciples in Nasik had a strong belief that their dreams indicated some special spiritual progress and were most anxious to recount them to anyone who would listen.

Baba lovingly agreed to listen to these dreams and discuss them and arranged for everyone to meet each morning at 5:30 in the sitting room. Delia and I, who confessed to having no dreams of any kind that we remembered, were told that instead of entering the discussion we were to brush Baba's hair and massage His scalp. For us this was wonderful. What were dreams compared with the pleasure of brushing Baba's beautiful hair and, with our fingertips, massaging His scalp. His head was an amazing shape. Even now my hands can remember how it was formed.

Every now and then while the dream session was going on, He would place His first finger on some spot that He felt had been neglected and it was immediately given extra treatment. Delia and I were so occupied with our job that we did not always hear all the dreams, but I do remember one morning an anguished voice saying, "Last night, Baba, I dreamt that I came to the edge of the great void, but I was afraid to jump in. Next time, Baba, push me in, push me in." Baba, looking suitably impressed, agreed to do so. Another one announced that she had dreamed that her head was a glass ball, and dear old Will Backett said meekly that in a dream he had looked at his own arm and knew that it was Baba's arm.

Delia and I certainly had no reason to bemoan our dreamless condition.

These sessions did not go on for more than two or three weeks, but they certainly brought certain facets of the ego up to the surface for all of us. This, explained Baba, must happen before the ego-facets can be destroyed.

The War Years

Don't try to understand Me.
My depth is unfathomable.
Just love Me.

MEHER BABA

Third Journey to India

When Baba left Cannes in 1937 to return to India with his party of close disciples, both Eastern and Western, He sent for me and told me to go to England; and since He had some work for me to do, I was for the time being to remain there. He put into my charge a young Indian boy, Faloo by name. He was the son of Rustom and Freni, Mehera's sister. I was to arrange for the boy to go to one of the English public schools, find a pleasant home where he might go for the holidays, in fact look after him and see things went happily for him while he was being educated.

It turned out, however, that this was not the important job, although the second and really important job could not have been carried out if the first one had not existed. In 1939 I received a letter from Baba dated July 4th, a few weeks before the outbreak of World War II.

This letter is still in my possession, although I cannot imagine how it survived the beginning of World War II. Practically everything else I had went.

The letter follows:

M. S. Irani
Meherabad, Ahmednagar
4th July 1939

Dearest Margaret and Delia,

The following contents are according to Baba's instructions and orders.

(1) If war breaks out involving England then you,

Margaret and Delia, come immediately to me here. You come any way that is best: *by air or by boat;* via America and Pacific; or by Africa *or* by boat from London, or from whatever port you find the most suitable.

(2) Christina and Minta can also come if they would like. Baba would love both of them to come. But for you and Delia there is no option. Once again, if war should break out and England be brought into it, then you and Delia must come to me in India immediately. This is my order.

All my Love,
M. S. Irani

I did not know what to make of this letter. At that time few people seemed to be convinced that war was inevitable. Neville Chamberlain, then Prime Minister of England, had paid a visit to Hitler and based on that visit believed that there would be no war.

Therefore when war did break out, the shock was tremendous.

On the night that the announcement was made by Chamberlain on the wireless, the next speaker after the prime minister gave a list of "may nots," and among them was that no one was to leave England!

Minta and Christina did not wish to go to India.

Delia, who was most anxious to obey Baba and go to India, had too many difficulties in the way to achieve this.

She had no excuse such as a tea plantation or a husband in the Indian army to offer the passport officials, and I could not offer to share Faloo—my only hope— with her. No official in his right mind would have believed that it could take two persons to escort a small boy to India. So no exit visa was forthcoming, and I was the only one left to get to India.

Every morning, feeling sick and terrible, I joined a queue, definitely about a mile long, and got into the passport office, only to be told that I could not leave the country. An occasional cable from Baba insinuating that I was not a good disciple did not help matters.

One morning, having followed a queue of unsuccessful persons, I arrived at a desk and waited meekly until the man in charge should condescend to notice me.

He looked up from his writing. His face changed from haughtiness to interest and to my surprise he said, "Where have I met you before?"

My reaction was immediate.

This must be Baba's "crack in the wall." A look of intense interest flowed over my face and I replied, "Yes, where was it?" Believe me, this young man and I carried on an idiotic conversation about some completely mythical meeting. At a dance? (I never went to dances but was prepared to have been to thousands.) A Labour Party reunion? etc., etc.

Finally the queue behind me got restless and began quite rightly objecting to this conversation.

The official, feeling that after all this "union of souls" he should really help me, courteously conducted me to some V.I.P.

By this time my hand had got firmly into the "crack in the wall." The V.I.P. was slightly stupid. This does not mean that he did not know his job. Therefore when I brought Faloo into the picture—I had his passport— and suggested that it would not be good at this point to offend Indian persons by not allowing this young child proper escort and care to get him safely home, he began to agree with me, and between us we managed to work up an atmosphere of Rule Britannia, and he gave me a visa to go to India!

So far, so good.

Then came the problem of passages to India. All the large steamship offices were frankly rude. Only Army officers and important government officials were allowed to fly. So?

This time America came to the rescue. The young man in charge of an American travel agency somewhere near Piccadilly Circus was friendly. He told me to go home, pack and be ready to go anywhere he told me at any given time. I felt slightly skeptical but promised to do as he said.

I was wrong. Within ten days he telephoned me, telling me to go the next night to Liverpool, and to fetch the tickets from him the following morning.

He had managed to book two berths on a boat supposedly sailing within the next few days.

The next day I fetched Faloo up from the country, paid the agency, and that night took off in the pitch dark on an unpleasant journey to Liverpool.

No lights anywhere, no one to see us off and the worst thing, no possibility of communicating with Baba to let Him know we had started. We were held up in Liverpool for four days. Finally we did reach the docks.

By this time I was decidedly nervous about the passport situation. It was all very well to talk about Faloo to the London officials but to show him to customs officers who were on the alert to stop anyone who should not leave the country was a different story. He was taller than I was and looked perfectly competent to get on a boat and take himself to India. Just as I feared. A most disagreeable customs officer looked at the passports and said with a very Scottish accent, "And where is the little boy?" I pointed to Faloo, whom I had kept in the background. He looked and of course said, "That little boy could take himself to Inda."

At that point I was in a quandary. Two orders— (1) "Don't tell lies" (2) "Get to India"—met head-on, and I lied. I looked terribly important, took a risk and said, "I have special permission from the Home Office to take this child to India."

Strangely enough, he accepted this statement and did not ask to see papers. He was, however, rather nasty. He took practically all my available cash and made me send it back to my London bank. Fortunately for me, having had a good upbringing on detective stories, I had put a ten-pound note under the inner sole of each of my shoes. It would just cover incidental expenses.

We went on board and, with three other ships which were with us to make a small convoy, swung around in the Mersey for four days. Our boat, supposedly in charge of the sailing, had on board an admiral and one anti-aircraft gun on the afterdeck. In the case of an attack by German submarines, which were making the Irish Sea a danger spot for ordinary shipping, I could not feel that either the admiral or his gun would be of much help.

Finally we left the haven of the Mersey and steamed out onto a sea charged with danger.

As I said, the worst thing about our situation was that I had lost any physical contact with Baba. It had of course been impossible to let Him know on what boat we had sailed. Everything was hush-hush.

We, the passengers, were told nothing. At night the

sea was dark, the sky was dark, no lights on the ship and in the distance there was occasionally the booming of guns. We slept in our clothes. At the end of several days, apparently having tacked backwards and forwards and criss-cross in the Irish Sea, rumor on board had it that we had got as far south as the Bristol Channel, usually a few hours' steaming from Liverpool. At that point, so we heard, the submarines had been forced to return to Germany to refuel, and we then went full speed ahead and reached the comparative safety of the Bay of Biscay.

By the time we reached the Mediterranean, the convoy had grown to about 25 ships, and the rule followed was to travel at the pace of the slowest boat.

There were at that time no signs of submarines in that neighborhood, but the French sent naval ships and airplanes to guard us. When we reached the entrance to the Suez Canal they turned and steamed back. The war had not yet reached this part of the world.

It was on the next part of the journey that the problem of communicating with Baba loomed quite insolubly into the foreground. No one seemed to know for which Indian port we were making. Rumor named places as far apart as Calcutta and Ceylon. The small sum of money with which I had been left could certainly not take Faloo and me anywhere near to Bangalore, and there was no way of communicating with anyone in India. It was like living in a vacuum. A black one, if there is such a thing. Finally we were told that the boat would stop in Ceylon.

In the meantime Delia had conveyed to Baba the fact that we had sailed, and as near as she could find out, the date of sailing.

Baba had got in touch with Thomas Cook's, who verified the sailing and gave an approximate time for the arrival in Ceylon.

He sent a charming old Indian disciple to meet us. He took the remains of my money away from me to help pay our fares to Bangalore.

So I went penniless to my Master, whose loving welcome wiped out everything that had happened in the effort to get to Him.

It was seven years before I again left Him.

About Books

S ince I was the last arrival at the Bangalore
ashram, all the jobs had been given out. So at
first I was just an outsider, hovering on the edges
of an already integrated system of work.

After a time Baba righted this situation, and one of
the things He gave me to do during evening sessions
with Him was to read aloud the war news as given in
the local newspaper. This order, however, had one
enormous difficulty. Mehera was still going through
the difficult period when she was not allowed to either
see a man or hear a man's name. Baba therefore told me
that while reading He wished me to substitute for any
man's name the term "So-and-So."

The readings turned out to be un-understandable
to everyone. Instead of Churchill or Hitler, the un-
meaningful "So and So" cropped up. The worst of it
was that all my fellow disciples seemed to blame me,
and after the readings they were mildly sarcastic. Baba
seemed to watch everyone's face to see how they were
taking it. Finally one evening He explained to Mehera
that since He was there it would be quite all right for
her to hear these names, and I was told to read the
names as written.

Reading aloud in the evenings became gradually
over the years a big affair. Since no money was spent on
them, books were not easy to obtain. Delia de Leon was
our chief mainstay. She mailed books every week or

two. These were in my charge, and on the bus tours my bedding roll was a cumbersome mess with these books.

First of all, we went through a course of Sherlock Holmes. This was followed by a great many of the Agatha Christie stories. Baba seemed enchanted by her main detective, Poirot. Following Christie came P. G. Wodehouse. I never felt that some of the Indian women quite appreciated his very English jokes, but they did seem to enjoy the ridiculous situations in which his characters found themselves. Baba got the jokes and enjoyed the hilarity caused by the doings of Lord Emsworth and his prize pig, the Empress of Blandings Castle.

This period was followed by the doings of Nero Wolfe and the humorous Archie. I believe that these two creations of Rex Stout became Baba's prime favorites. Other detective stories filled in the gaps, but the foregoing writers definitely gave Baba the most pleasure.

Very often, just as were reaching the climax of a story and it was certain that the next chapter would solve the mystery, Baba would smile sweetly and announce that it was bedtime; and although I had charge of the books, even sleeping on them when I was too tired to take them out of my bedding roll, I was not allowed to open the book after closing it, until the next session with Baba. And—well, you know all about obedience.

Years later, after my arrival in America and certain dancers were beginning to love Baba, I received a letter from Him saying that He would like to have every book that Rex Stout had ever written. This was not altogether easy to manage. Rex Stout had been writing and publishing his books for many years, and several of them were already out of print. But I was aided by young dancers, who went on tour with different companies and could investigate many secondhand provincial bookshops; and by an important concert agent who loved Baba and insisted that an exclusive shop where he spent a great deal of money should look around; plus willing searchers in the secondhand bookshops around 14th Street (New York); and even by Foyles of London—a famous secondhand bookshop in Charing Cross Road—which produced a couple.

Every one of the books that Rex Stout had written up to that time was found, parcelled, and sent to the dancers' beloved Master. It was fortunate for these young dancers that they were able to do some small personal service for Baba.

When the Tolkein trilogy appeared on the market, I at once sent the first volume to India. No time wasted. By return mail I was told to send the other two volumes immediately—which I did.

Dance Teacher

I n 1939, soon after arriving in India, one of Baba's close followers, Kerawalla, a good but rather narrow-minded man, chose to object to my presence in the ashram as one of Baba's mandali.

He told Baba—thinking I am sure that I was a belly dancer, or a not properly clad night club performer, and forgetting the beauty of the Indian religious dances traditionally introduced into the world by the god Shiva himself—that it would do immeasurable harm to Baba's reputation in the outside world if I were allowed to remain with His close disciples.

I do not know what passed between them but the next thing was that Baba asked me if anyone in London would write a short account of my work in dancing. At Baba's wish I wrote to Cyril Beaumont, dance critic of the *London Observer* and author of many learned books on dancing, and asked him if he would do this for me.

In a short time, in spite of his disapproval of my going to India, he wrote a most kind article about my teaching and choreography, and mailed it to India. I gave it to Baba, who showed it to Kerawalla. He was not moved by it, and continued to urge Baba to remove me from the ashram.

To bring matters to a head, Baba then informed me that He wished me to open a school of dancing in Bangalore. I was horrified. The few children in Bangalore were mostly the offspring of British Army officers, who might consider sending their children—about once a week—for lessons in ballroom dancing and the social behavior that went with it, and my knowledge of this branch of dancing was almost nil.

A few days after this bombshell, Baba took me with Ramjoo to inspect a small building which He intimated would be the scene of the proposed Bangalore dancing activities.

The front door opened straight onto an unattractive, not very large room which, to add to its total ineligibility, had a concrete floor.

Baba stretched out His hands and made Ramjoo ask me what I thought of it.

I turned to explain that, without endangering the limbs of pupils, no form of dancing could be taught on such a floor; and, in the case of ballet, bad cases of tendonitis would most certainly result.

Baba beamingly pushed all this aside and showed delight with the place, and made signs that the room would be painted, and that the outside of the building would be enlivened by electric signs. Rather like a night club.

At this point, although I felt that the room was impossible and always would be, I gave up and joined with Baba and Ramjoo in planning to make the building into a vehicle for Baba's wish.

Some strange built-in tables which took up valuable space would have to be removed, exercise bars connected to the walls, and the floor covered with linoleum under which there would have to be pads.

After some discussion, Baba made a happy sign to indicate that everything was settled, the changes would be made and, as soon as possible, the school would be opened.

What happened I do not know, but after that day I never heard another word about the project!

I have always felt, however, that Kerawalla must have been so overcome by Baba's persistence in backing up dancing to the extent of proposing to open a school that he changed his mind about the evils of dancing and, that being all along what Baba had wanted, to my intense relief the "Bangalore School of Dance" died before it was born.

Connection with Australia

I n 1932 Baba met and embraced an Australian pupil of mine. One day she came to me with a story that she had had a vision of Baba standing quietly for a time in her bedroom and then disappearing. Well, that's as it may be . . .

Some time after my arrival in India in 1939, some Australian teachers of dancing, hearing I was in India and feeling no doubt that the fare would be cheaper than from England, invited me to go to Australia to conduct ballet examinations and to give some lessons.

I showed this letter to Baba. He seemed delighted and said that of course I must go. I was not particularly elated.

I had no clothes to speak of but, obeying Baba's orders, I started negotiations with the society of teachers. It was not as easy as it had seemed. Even though the war had not spread to the Pacific, there were certain passage difficulties. For instance, when I did manage to obtain a passage it turned out that I should arrive during the summer vacation in Australia. But preparations went on. Baba had the local tailor make me a suit and drove me to continue the correspondence. Elizabeth dived into her wardrobe and came up with a beautiful blue evening gown for me.

Finally, when war broke out in the Pacific and the project was rendered impossible, Baba asked me to find out whether, if He sent a large package of writings about His teachings, someone would be willing to distribute them for Him. I wrote at once, asking this, and a reply came, written by the woman who had had the vision of Him, saying she would be happy to do this.

A few minutes with Baba, an embrace, a vision ... then several years later Baba was able to use her to make this needed link with Australia.

Amboli

I n the early days of the war, Baba took the group to a small house in Amboli. It was on the edge of a forest, a wild place with tigers, and it seemed to specialize in a most unpleasant snake, the krait. This small creature had the habit of dropping from a tree onto a passerby, who never knew it or anything else.

There was not room for the whole party in the main house. Some managed to get into the servants' quarters, while a few slept on a verandah.

Irene Billo was taken ill, and Baba and Donkin decided that she had typhoid. I was told to nurse her. My instructions were to give her some medicine at intervals and do what I could about washing her and such.

The strangest order came from Baba. He gave me a cake of Lifebuoy soap and told me that every half hour I was to wash my hands with this disinfectant, and every now and then Baba, looking radiant, would appear on the other side of the compound and make the motions of hand washing.

During the night, if Irene were sick, I had to take the used utensils and go into the forest and empty them. Here Norina showed me the greatest kindness. She would always come with me and carry the hurricane lamp. She could not, of course, have prevented a nocturnally inclined krait from dropping on my head, but her presence was most comforting and naturally she also took the krait risk. In the end it turned out that

Irene did not have typhoid. She was just sick. I wonder what Baba and Donkin were up to!

One day we were all called into a kind of living room where we were presented to a Rani who had a country house in the neighborhood. She was charming and invited us all to tea. Clothes to take tea with a Rani were a difficulty. They always came out of our bedding rolls crumpled and messy—and most of us had to spend the morning stroking out a dress with damp hands, the nearest we could get to ironing.

We arrived at her palace. She had her guards lined up on either side of the avenue. Baba looked wonderful, striding full of life, love and energy through these guards, who presented arms as He passed along.

The Rani gave us a delicious tea and took the trouble to speak to each of us separately.

One night Nadine Tolstoy and I, who were sleeping out on the verandah, noticed prowling around the compound what, in the semi-light, looked like an enormous dog.

It was not clear to us what the animal was, but since there were many tigers in the neighboring forest we had our suspicions. We lay still, thinking of Baba and scarcely breathing. After a time the creature went away, and when sufficient time had elapsed, Nadine sat up and said dramatically in her deep Russian voice, "That was no dog."

One afternoon Baba took us for a walk along a high plateau. It was comfortably broad and jutted out from the main road. It had enormous drops on either side and we could see small villages far below.

Since I have a very bad head for heights, I kept well in the center of this projection. It then narrowed to a rocky footpath leading to another plateau and I decided that I would not cross it. Baba, however, decided otherwise. From the other side of the foot path, a few yards in length, He stretched out loving hands to me. I went forward, keeping my eyes on Him, and my head behaved beautifully. When I reached the other side Baba took hold of my dress at the back of my neck and held my head out over the precipice. I caught a glimpse far below of a small village, and then hurriedly closed my eyes. This did not please Baba. He pulled my head up and with the first and second fingers of each hand opened His own eyes very wide, indicating that I should not close mine. Then once more He hung my head over the precipice. This time I managed to keep my eyes open.

I have not since been in the same situation, so I do not know if a cure was effected.

Jaipur

Late one moonlit evening the group arrived at a house just on the outskirts of Jaipur. Since it was too late to organize and arrange living quarters, Baba sent word that we were to take our bedding rolls and sleep for the one night wherever we felt inclined. I went up a staircase, the walls and ceiling of which were black with insects, and found myself on a flat, moonlit roof. There was a small glass shelter, and since no one else had discovered this staircase, I promptly spread out my bedding roll, went to bed and slept happily, waking at intervals to murmur, "How wonderful to be alone." I think that until that night I had had no realization of what a discipline it was never to be alone.

The next day, Nadine, Irene and I were given a room so small that when our bedding rolls were spread out, they exactly covered the floor space. At this time my two roommates were going through a year's disciplinary silence. This definitely was also a discipline for the rest of us. There was the learning of the deaf and dumb alphabet, and having to be careful never to get caught in a corner where the silent ones, once we were trapped, would usually feel inspired to tell the victim the story of their lives. When told letter by letter, lives seem endless. Even today a mention of Zurich brings up a picture of the best-laid sewer pipes in Europe! A source of great pride to Irene.

It was arranged that we should take turns in

sweeping the floor of our room and keeping it tidy. The first morning Irene did the chores, and afterwards Nadine's fingers indignantly told me that Irene had finished by sweeping the dust under her, Nadine's, bedding roll. The next day Irene came to me and spelt out the same story about Nadine.

The third day, knowing that there could be no hope for my reputation as a sweeper, I swept the dust under their bedding rolls and later saw them together, indignantly wagging their fingers about my sins.

Donkin was there with the group for a time. I imagine he must have spent a fortune getting from different military hospitals in various parts of India in order to be, even for a short time, wherever Baba might be. His devotion was such.

During this visit he seemed extremely upset and professionally angry to find not far from the house an open sewer ditch flowing peacefully and poisonously towards the place of its ultimate destruction. He demanded inoculations for the entire group. As soon, however, as Baba said that everything was in His hands, he accepted this and left the matter there.

Numbers of black-faced monkeys lived on the property, and in spite of their wistful charm, they were definitely tiresome, sometimes even snatching food from our plates and then vanishing rapidly. Elephants and occasionally camels ambled along the road which passed the end of the garden. At other times, the weaving of a long piece of silky material having been completed and needing to be dried, would be floated along the street about shoulder height by runners holding the edges. One day everyone in the city, including the head of the city government, went out to celebrate some special festival by flying kites. It was a wonderful sight. The sky when filled with flying beauty—all colors, shapes and sizes—was hypnotically pleasing. Baba seemed to enjoy this scene.

On one side of the grounds surrounding the house was a tomb in which rested the bones of a sixth plane saint. One day Baba took me over to look at this strange small erection and explained that a strong emanation of Love was still flowing from it. I, however, did not feel this, I think because in His presence, Baba's own emanation of Love was so strong that one could be aware of no other.

The Tiger

lthough moderately intelligent human beings, Baba's early Western disciples found that, in spite of the love for Him that He had awakened in their hearts, there were certain difficulties in talking easily and naturally to Him.

Baba's wish was for us to feel no self-conscious barrier, and He broke a great deal of this nonsense by telling us, "You cannot come to my level, so I have to come to yours."

This certainly made matters easier, and we were able to react to His Love in a less difficult manner. We were no longer afraid to say or do the wrong thing.

One day while we were happily sitting round Him, He told us that one day He would call us to India, and that we should stay with Him for the rest of our lives.

As were digesting this statement, someone chirped up, "Baba what shall we do if we meet a tiger?" About on a par with asking what to do if we should meet a buffalo in America.

But Baba took the question seriously, and spelt out the following on His alphabet board: "If you ever meet a tiger, stand perfectly still and inwardly repeat my name."

Years later, Baba had his whole group of by this time rather battered disciples staying with Him in Mahableshwar. The house was on a slight elevation from where one could look down onto a forest which stretched for miles across the country.

The British, mostly army officers, used the forest for tiger shooting expeditions.

With the group at this time were some boys whom Baba was training to serve Him, either out in the world or in a closer ashram life. They seemed quite wonderful boys, learning early to follow the path of Love and Obedience.

One of their main jobs was at night to patrol the house where the women might be sleeping.

In the early morning in some districts, as many as seven or eight dead snakes could be found stretched out near the entrance to the house where the women slept.

One night, two of the boys on duty felt that something was wrong. They turned on their flashlights, and there prowling at no great distance from them was a fierce-looking tiger.

They were so well trained that even the terror of seeing this frightening apparition did not make them forget Baba's order about dealing with this particular situation.

They turned off their lights, became frozen into immobility, and immediately started to repeat inwardly, "Baba, Baba, Baba."

After some time the fear began to abate and they felt safer. At this point one of them turned on his flashlight, just in time to see the animal leaping over the wall and going back into the forest.

Outside Goa

Baba and His disciples were held up for one day on the outskirts of Goa (Portuguese territory). The entrance papers were not in order.

The *dak* bungalow was quite pleasant, and everything was peaceful until Gaimai, from the kindness of her heart, offered to cook the midday meal. A wave of horror passed through Norina and me. Gaimai was an excellent cook. The Easterners loved her food, which was probably the hottest and spiciest I have ever eaten. But both Norina and I had stomachs that refused to accept that kind of food. We got together, decided to eat outside near some bushes, and surreptitiously empty our plates behind them. It seemed better to go hungry for a few hours than to suffer the misery caused by that kind of food.

At lunch time, feeling that our problem was solved, we stepped happily into the improvised dining room, only to find that it wasn't. Baba, looking radiant, had appeared and announced that He wished to serve the food to His disciples. And the rule was that any food served or given by the Master must be eaten. He seemed to think that I must be especially hungry and, with a loving smile, placed an extra spoonful on my plate.

Norina and I did not look at each other. Our plan had failed. The results were as expected.

Choice

At one time or another, many of the disciples came up against the difficulty of a situation in which two strict orders conflicted and an immediate choice had to be made as to the right course of action.

One extremely hot afternoon at Meherabad on the Hill, a strange health crisis arose. One after another, with no warning, everyone began to vomit. After an hour or two, nearly everyone lay weak and moaning on a bed or just stretched out on the ground at the point of attack.

The two doctors in attendance on the ashram at that time, Donkin and Nilu, were sent for and they came up the Meherabad Hill looking white and frightened. They knew, but we did not, that cholera was rife in Ahmednagar.

At this time, Baba was in seclusion in a room on the far side of the compound. He had left orders that He was on no account to be disturbed.

On the other hand, the doctors had a permanent order to see that nothing untoward should happen to the women's group.

Horrified at the situation, they disregarded the seclusion orders and without delay sent a message to Baba.

He did not send a verbal answer, but almost immediately the vomiting eased down and finally stopped, although for a few days those who had been attacked were weak and listless.

It seems that the doctors had made the right choice.

Mango Ice Cream

While Baba and His group of disciples were staying for a few days at the *dak* bungalow in a small village, He unexpectedly gave us an afternoon with Him. At Mehera's wish an unusual treat of mango ice cream was made and Baba served it to us. It was no one's birthday, and as with many of the happiest times with Baba, it seemed to happen completely out of the blue.

Norina was not present. Baba had sent her and Donkin to do certain work for Him in a large town some little distance away. Meanwhile, we were having a happy time with Baba.

Then suddenly He looked at me and told me to pray out loud for the safety of Norina and Donkin. Rather taken aback, I lost my head and started: "Dear unknown God." Baba clapped His hands to stop me and spelt out, "What do you mean, unknown God?" I meekly said I had thought He meant I should pray to "God the Beyond." He then indicated that I should start again. This time I said, "Dear God," and looked at Baba, then continued "You have told us to ask for nothing, but with your special permission, I ask you for the safe journey and return of our dear friends, Norina and Donkin. Amen."

Baba looked happy and served me another small portion of ice cream.

Norina and Donkin returned quite safely.

Tiger on the Porch

*L*ate at night, during one of the Indian bus tours, we stopped at a *dak* bungalow, got our bedding rolls from the top of the bus, and started looking round for places to sleep.

It was not a large building, and by the time I had rescued my night kit, I found that the rooms were crowded and decided in spite of the sound of tigers in the offing—there were always night watchmen—to sleep on the porch.

I spread out my mattress and was just about to get ready to crawl into it when the door on my right side opened. Out came Eruch and I found that this was the entrance to Baba's room. Eruch then informed me that no one was allowed to sleep outside Baba's door and that I should move away at once.

I rolled up my mattress and was just moving away when Eruch, who had in the meantime returned to Baba, came out again with a message from Him that for this once I might sleep near His door. So on Baba's doorstep, with a lullaby from distant tigers, I almost at once fell into a sleep of deep exhaustion, which sometime during the night brought me a strange dream. It was as if I were lying awake when the door of Baba's room opened and out came Baba. He was no longer the Baba that I knew, but was a large tiger walking on His hind legs. But the face was Baba's face.

He proceeded to walk round my bed, opening His

mouth and waving His front paws at me, and in the dream this seemed perfectly natural and not frightening. After a short time, He went back through the open door which closed after Him.

The next day I told Baba of this dream. He seemed delighted and indicated that the next time it happened He would eat me. It never happened again and I am still uneaten.

Journey to Quetta—1940

The bus trip through central India had not been a comfortable one. The heat was intense. New tires were needed. Several times the drivers had had to turn us out on the road—sometimes where there were trees and sometimes not—while they blew up the tires or changed them. And it was an exhausted crowd that arrived in Multan in northern India, where we stayed for a short time before crossing the mountains to go to Quetta. We found Multan was cold, and out of our bedding rolls we produced whatever warm clothes we had brought.

As it happened, one of the only really nice garments I managed to bring to India was a lavender-blue woolen coat. The evening of our arrival, Baba called us to tell us His plans for crossing the mountain pass leading to Quetta. As I came into the room, He looked at my coat and made signs of approval, then turned to Norina, whose clothes almost invariably came from the name dressmakers of the day—Worth, Chanel, etc.—and spelt on the board, "Why do you not dress as well as Margaret does?"

There was quite a silence in the room. Everyone knew the difference between clothes off a peg and the other kind; in fact at intervals we had heard all this from Norina, who was shocked into silence by this subtle twisting of values.

The passes through the mountains after the winter

season were only just open and were still dangerous. Not from the weather, but parties of brigands had been descending from the hills and killing the season's first travelers. Baba was adamant about our going that way. He had new tires put on the bus and arranged for most of the men to go to Quetta by train! The women were to go in the bus, while the girls would travel in the car with Him.

The first place at which we stopped for a short time was a large village by the name of Dehra Duzi Khan. The villagers seemed amazed, and stood round the bus staring and pressing their faces on the windows to get a look at the busload of women. I am sure that messages were sent straight off to their cousins, the brigands, about such strange travelers.

After some hours of driving we came to the river Jumna. It looked about a quarter of a mile wide and had to be crossed by the most unsafe-looking pontoon bridge. Not a nice firm structure, such as an army might have built, but a very wobbly affair, seemingly of planks run across boats.

Baba's car crossed easily enough, but the bus . . . ! A poor little man, evidently some kind of bridgemaster, pointed to a notice saying that nothing weighing over one ton would be allowed to cross. The bus, with all the bedding rolls on top, which in any case gave it a top-heavy look, and all the women inside, certainly exceeded that. Donkin, who was driving, became all British officer and ordered the man to let us pass. So, leaving the man wringing his hands, we went down a sloping river bank and onto the bridge.

The boats rocked from side to side, and inside the bus all the older women got out their prayer beads, and the name of Baba rang through the bus. Halfway across, a rain and windstorm came down the river. Not too bad, but enough to add to the rocking of the bus. The worst of it was that we knew that if the bus rocked sideways into the water there was no hope for any of us. We could not get out. There were only small entrance doors which could not have been opened. It was the greatest relief to reach the other bank.

After some more bumpy driving through a forest, the bus arrived at a small building on the side of the road, which turned out to be a British Army outpost.

A red-faced colonel came to look at the bus and, at the sight of its cargo of women, looked as if he might at any moment be seized with a fit of apoplexy.

On the hillside near at hand was a *dak* bungalow where we slept that night and the next. All the time we were there the colonel, I suppose fearing danger for us, kept his men working and digging very close to the house.

The next day the weather changed to a kind of drizzle, and there was nothing to occupy the time. I was sitting gloomily on the edge of a low wall when Baba came along and sat beside me. He sat there for a minute or two and then, to my surprise, spelt on His board: "If I asked you to, would you die for Me?"

This shook me up. After a pause I said, "I should like to answer that question truthfully and not just emotionally. Will you give me half an hour to settle it in my mind?"

Baba went away and at the end of half an hour He returned, sat down and stretched out His hands questioningly. I was thankful to be able to say "yes" and to have no doubts in my mind.

Early the next morning, we climbed into the bus and jogged along until we came to a wide plain surrounded by mountains and filled with small huts. We stopped there for some little time. The villagers welcomed Baba vociferously. I think He must have visited them on the previous day. They crowded round Him, telling Him they would like to show Him their treasured racehorses. Baba, absolutely shining with loving interest and acting as if it were the one thing He would wish to do, had them bring out the animals and, urged on by His vitality and interest, they raced the horses along a length of railed-off ground. They were a pathetic set of animals, but the happiness that Baba gave these poor people, and the way they were drawn to Him was a kind of miracle. It was a contact with Divine Love. They felt it but did not know it.

The village itself consisted of small huts, out of which the women, with the lower part of their faces covered with a *yashmak*, practically crawled to carry food to their menfolk, who were obviously their masters. I do not think that women's lib would have approved such behavior.

Then, across the plain from out of the entrance to the mountain pass tore a car which turned out to be the British mail. On the roof, cross-legged, sat a soldier in a white tunic with a red fez on his head and with the longest rifle I had ever seen stretched across his knees. It turned out that on its return journey we were to join this outfit, and it would escort us through the danger zone.

Another soldier of the same type appeared from somewhere and got onto the front of our bus. Baba and the girls squeezed into the bus with us, and at a sign from the mail van, both vehicles took off to cross the plain towards the pass. Somehow I don't think anyone took the danger seriously. It was too much like something from the early cinema days, when incidents like this were usually accompanied by a gallop on the piano. I could almost hear it.

As we drove through the pass, Baba kept pointing out rocky paths where the brigands had, the week before or two days before, descended and demolished a few travelers. This went on for quite some time. Then suddenly it was discovered that we had lost the mail car! No one knew where it had disappeared. We did not see it again, so were really on our own, except for the man with the rifle.

Soon after we had arrived at the end of the pass and were jogging along quite comfortably, we came to a riverbed. It was wide and had no water in it, but was not firm enough to take the bus; therefore, about halfway across we stopped suddenly, having sunk into the sand.

We all got out to lighten the weight. Our guard stood with his rifle ready to fire at the first sign of any attackers. After a time, some planks were brought and the bus was released to start again on its journey.

We arrived in the late afternoon at our scheduled night stop, and as we drove into the village a British Army sergeant cycled up to us and said casually that we were late and that they had been thinking of sending out a search party to look for us.

We arrived at a *dak* bungalow. It then turned out that our food was running short and that supper was to be omitted. Baba came round with a box of Frear's cream biscuits and gave us each one.

The next thing that happened shows, I believe, why

we had not been attacked. Baba had communicated with the head of the village where we spent the morning, offering to take his son to Ahmednagar and have him trained as a film operator in the local cinema. The man accepted, and this fine-looking boy had traveled with us, sitting in front with the driver. I imagine that the father had sent a stern message to the hills saying that we were not to be attacked.

Although one biscuit had constituted our supper, a more substantial meal was produced for the boy. One of the Western women must have taken it to him because he refused it angrily, saying, "I will not be fed by white-faced pigs," and demanded that he should be sent back home. Having served his purpose, he was sent back the next day.

The following morning the bus went on to Quetta, and this time the roads were civilized and safe.

Foundy - 1940

In Quetta I was sometimes allowed, if Elizabeth were going out on business for Baba, to go with her in the car. One day she had to go to the railway station. While there, she spotted a large black dog. It was wandering miserably about, hunting for food. It looked like one of the poor dogs so often abandoned by his master when a regiment moved from one place to another.

Elizabeth's love for animals could not take this. She enticed him into the car, took him back to the place where we were living with Baba and was given permission to keep him and take him back to Meherabad. He was named Foundy.

On the way going south to Ahmednagar, Elizabeth drove Baba's car, and the animal fell to my lot to look after in the bus. I loved him, but in the bus my love faded somewhat. There was definitely no room for him, and he had to sprawl across my knees. In the Indian heat, this was no pleasure. It was like having a fur rug.

One morning as we were waiting to get in the bus and I was standing with my dog friend on a leash, gloomily thinking of the uncomfortable day ahead, Baba suddenly appeared, walking towards the bus. He stopped when He saw me and asked if I should like to take the dog and sit on the front seat with the driver. I thankfully accepted the offer.

A few minutes later the driver came along, looked

at me preparing to mount to the seat next to his, and reacted strongly against this. He did not like dogs. This man was not one of Baba's regular disciples, but since he was the father of one of Baba's younger disciples and did not altogether approve of his son's determination to follow a spiritual path, it was Baba's wish that he should not be annoyed.

At this moment Baba returned and, seeing the crisis, turned to me fiercely, as if I were some kind of criminal, and spelt out, "Who told you that you might sit with the driver?" And from deep inside me I knew what to say. I said, "No one, Baba."

Baba turned towards the man and stretched out His hands as if to say disparagingly, "Disciples!" And the dog and I turned and went to our appointed spot in a hot world.

Cables and Links

For a few weeks Baba and His group settled into a bungalow at Panchgani which stood back from the road leading up to Mahableshwar. It was there that the beloved and wonderful mast, Chatti Baba, suddenly decided that the time had come for him to leave Baba and return to southern India.

One morning he started off down the hilly road, ostensibly to return home. He managed to cover quite a few miles before some of Baba's disciples overtook him and brought him back in a car. Baba agreed that he should go and sent him off properly equipped for the long journey and accompanied by one of the mandali. I have never seen so much sadness in Baba's face as when Chatti Baba's car went down the hill.

During that period at Panchgani, Baba dictated to me a series of letters and cables to be sent to Elizabeth concerning a proposed trip to America with some of the disciples. As a good secretary should, I made copies of all these. Unfortunately, just before we left Panchgani, Baba sent Chanji to ask for these copies for the archives. Of the following cable, I had two copies, and it seems sufficient to show Baba making links with certain world events.

Cable from Baba in Panchgani to Elizabeth in America (late 1941):

Myself and Upasani met Oct. 9th after 23 years and momentous spiritual decisions necessitate my speaking any day between Feb. 5th 1942 and Feb. 5th 1943 and also crossing ocean middle December latest (1941). Funds insufficient must cancel America. Therefore definitely prefer Honolulu, Philippines, or any place in the Pacific incurring less expensive fare.

On December 7, 1941, the eyes of a horrified world were drawn to Honolulu and the Japanese attack on Pearl Harbor. Most of the places mentioned in the cable were seized by the Japanese.

Every evening the party, including the servants, gathered around Baba, who would at intervals point to someone and demand a short story, a limerick, or even a poem. This was all very well for a short time, but then came a bad period when, having no reference books, but only a couple of ancient Reader's Digests and some overworked memories, things became rather sticky.

One evening He pointed to me and as a last hope I said feebly, "Shall I tell you a story I wrote in my early teens?" Everyone quite rightly looked pained, but Baba signed to me to do this, and out of His loving kindness seemed to enjoy it.

However, I let myself in for something. Baba then said that every evening He would give me a title and that the next evening I should present Him with a plot made from the given title. "Yussuf, the Yellow One" is the only title I remember.

My everyday job at this time was to sit out under a shady tree, armed with a lathi (a stick with a lead-loaded head) and to allow no unauthorized person to enter the gate. Since no one ever came, there was plenty of time to work out a plot that hopefully would amuse my Master.

Dehra Dun

One day while we were staying at Dehra Dun, Baba sent for me. I found Him sitting with Donkin, and they both looked at me most solemnly. Donkin rather overdid the solemnity, which made me suspect a hoax.

Baba then signalled to Donkin to say his piece, and he asked me if I were to be physically attacked by anyone, did I know of any ways to protect myself, or even how to kill an attacker. I was shocked, but said that I did. Baba signalled to me to enumerate them.

I mentioned a blow on the temple, provided one had a heavy enough instrument, and also the same treatment at the throat. The atmosphere grew more serious, and I was told that since at any time the Japanese might invade the northern part of India, I must train everyone in the art of self-defense. But more important than anything else, some system was to be devised for the special protection of Mehera.

Baba had ordered about a dozen lathis (short sticks with large heads filled with lead), and with these, every afternoon, I was to teach the servants how to protect themselves. There was only one thing to do in the face of such apparent craziness. I entered into the spirit of the thing and enjoyed it.

So every afternoon I taught the servants all I knew, including the fireman's lift, how to trip enemies who were running past by throwing a lathi between their legs, etc. The maids giggled quite a lot and took sly blows at each other, so that I was forced to have them make imitation lathis from newspapers. The other things were too dangerous.

The Westerners were very cold towards these proceedings, and did as little as they could get away with.

Arrangements for Mehera's safety were as follows. She herself would go onto the roof. The narrow stairway leading to the roof was to be guarded by alloted lathi-armed persons. Others would go to the doors and repel the invaders. Since there were not enough lathis to go round, these were to carry jars of pepper with which, hopefully, they would manage to blind the enemy!

Baba was very strict and insisted that all this should be practiced seriously. Strangely enough, a short time after these peculiar proceedings had run their course, the Indians in that part of the country near Dehra Dun, armed only with lathis, attacked certain British institutions, such as post offices, minor government offices and restaurants. They caused a certain amount of damage, but the whole thing was stamped out. Although I personally did not hear Baba say this, many disciples believed that He used the ashram to work things out that would afterwards happen in the outside world. Take this incident as you will.

A Scare in Mahableshwar

The following frightening incident happened in Mahableshwar while we were staying there with Baba.

The house was situated in a rather wild place with miles of open country around it. Baba gave the group permission to take daily walks over the hills, but with the proviso that no one should go alone. Just small groups all going at the same time.

Mehera and her close companions were also allowed the freedom of the countryside. One afternoon when Baba was away and we were exploring this wild, beautiful place, we came to a flat piece of ground on the top of a hill. It was covered with enormous roots, which looked very much like arrowroot. For most of us the idea of eating a piece did not enter our heads. Nebulous memories of childhood warnings against eating growing things we knew nothing about kept even the idea of sampling the roots away from most of us.

The group with Mehera was interested in the roots, and one of them, Carmen Massie, an elderly lady, took a large bite, chewed and swallowed it. Mehera, I believe, was in danger of swallowing some, but did not do so.

On reaching the house, Carmen Massie was taken desperately ill and seemed about to die. It was terrifying. There was no possibility of getting the doctor. The men were living in a house some distance away, and since it was now dark and no one knew where their house was situated, it was impossible to venture out over the hills to find them.

It was a dreadful time. The older Indian women brought out their prayer beads and continuously repeated Baba's name, and the rest kept their minds on Baba.

We were thankful when the night watchman arrived. He was immediately sent back over the hills to fetch Dr. Nilu. He came and, after examining Carmen Massie, found it impossible to diagnose the trouble. He looked pale, and confessed his ignorance of her strange symptoms.

Towards morning, Carmen Massie seemed slightly better, and after a few days she recovered. This was a miracle. For on inquiring about these roots among the local peasants, it turned out that if it were found necessary to kill any of their cattle, they were fed portions of this root, which would immediately cut the intestines into small pieces and throw them out of the body, causing instant death.

Irene's Dog

While I was nursing Irene during her bouts of catatonia, the group stayed for a few weeks in a house where Irene and I slept and lived at one side of the house in a verandah room, which had three walls and one side open to the outside air. Here we were joined by a stray dog.

The dog affected Irene very happily. When he was on the verandah, she felt more alive and the catatonia attacks were much less frequent. He had a special mat. We were not, however, allowed to feed him; his food was given him in the kitchen, but otherwise he was perfectly happy to spend much time sleeping on the mat.

Then came one of those unpleasant incidents. A certain woman—not a regular resident of the ashram— who did not like Westerners, lured the dog away to the other side of the house by giving him extra food, and was slightly difficult when, giving her the reason, I asked her not to.

It was not good to see my patient, at the defection of her dog friend, going back to more frequent collapses. Then fortunately, from my detective story education, I remembered learning that dog stealers would put anise powder into cuffs on their trouser legs and were then followed by dogs fascinated by this, to them, delicious smell.

I waited for an empty kitchen, raided the stores, found some anise, helped myself and covered the dog's mat with this tempting smell. The dog returned and nothing could afterwards tempt him to leave this delectable spot.

Journey to Lonavla

The end came to one of the periods spent in Dehra Dun. Baba announced that the party would be going for a short time to Lonavla, a hill country district not far from Bombay.

At that time I was looking after Irene Billo, who was suffering from catatonia, an illness in which the sufferer suddenly goes off into a state in which she cannot move any part of her body whatsoever, but is still aware of what goes on around her.

The journey started and we got safely as far as New Delhi with no collapse from Irene. Soon after we left that terminus, she fell into a trance-like condition, and at the first stop Dr. Nilu was summoned. Since Mehera was still in purdah and everyone was traveling in the same long compartment, Nilu's presence as he gave the injection caused a great deal of confusion.

At the next station Baba, feeling that enough was enough, turned us out, escorted by Nilu, with orders to follow by the next train. Just as the train drew into Lonavla station, Irene decided to have an attack. We pulled her out of the train and she lay flat on the platform.

The train was packed with soldiers who, at the sight of this pretty, fair-haired girl stretched out on the platform, came to the windows, got out on the platform, gave vent to cat-calls, and shouted all kinds of dubious remarks. Finally, when Nilu got out his instrument case and gave her an injection, there was almost a riot. It was a relief when some of the men disciples arrived with a chair to carry her and we left the station, accompanied by cheers and laughter.

Lonavla was one of the places where we were allowed to feed stray dogs, and every morning I shared my breakfast with a small, ugly, half-starved dog, who always wagged his tail in an effort to be cheerful. My witty fellow disciples called him "Mr. Craske."

With us on this trip was a woman who spent much time reading the lives of various saints and, not liking dogs, she one afternoon took a small stick and gave poor Mr. Craske a sharp blow, cutting him just above the eye.

I was still exhausted from the journey and looking after Irene, and was suffering from some severe bruises caused by a fall, and this was too much. I lost my temper, said what I thought of this woman, and finished up my verbal attack with: "And you read about saints in the morning and beat dogs in the afternoon!"

This was unforgivable and, since news went round the ashram like lightning, it reached Baba in no time. He sent for me and for everyone else who was free at the time, and in front of them pointed out my sins. Disgraced and humiliated, I crept away and, leaving Irene to her fate, retired under my mosquito net and cried and cried and cried.

I remember that the only thing I seemed to be crying about was that God had created the universe. No anger at all against Baba, only the unmanifest God. This went on for a least a day. At intervals Baba would send for me, look puzzled, and point out that other people had been scolded and they had not behaved like this. I remember saying, "You have pushed me down under the sands of the desert, and I'll stay there. Boo-hoo." After a time I came around, recovered my sanity, and resumed my charge of Irene.

About a week later, I was seated near a field of grain. The sun was shining and a soft breeze blowing, causing the gold of the grain to billow across the hillside in lovely consecutive waves, bringing back to me love for the beauty of God's creation. How dreadful if He had not sent out His creative waves of Love. We should never have existed and known Baba.

Men's Meeting in Meherabad

While the group was staying in Lonavla, Baba announced that He wished to have a meeting in Meherabad with men from all over India who had spent time with Him and had then been sent out into the world, there to continue their service to Him. For this event, the whole party was transferred to Meherabad, and preparations were put into action. It was then discovered that because of war conditions many of these men could not possibly get to Meherabad. Baba then arranged that those who lived within a reasonable distance of Meherabad should come, and that Baba would, when possible, make visits to different parts of India in order to connect up with the rest of the early disciples.

It was arranged that tents should be put up on the hill sloping down from the women's quarters to the men's quarters. These would supply places to sleep and eat and would make it easy for the poorer members to afford to come and once more for a short time be with their beloved Master.

December is a month when rain is not expected, but this time the unexpected happened. Torrents of rain descended and turned the hill into a place of mud and water that made it seem impossible that the reunion could take place. However, since it seemed that Baba had deeply wished for this meeting, His men disciples decided that this catastrophe should not prevent it from happening. They could not bear the idea that Baba should not have His wish. They all set to work, drained the hillside by mysterious means, got rid of the mud and, with the help of the December sun, made it possible to put up the tents and equip the place for these men to live in for a few days.

Just before the arrival of these guests, up on the hill in the women's quarters Baba made a few scathing remarks on my character and finished up by saying that He thought I should go down the hill and attend the meeting. Making it sound like a kind of punishment. No one else objected!

So at about 8:30 p.m. in the soft December sunlight I went down the hill to the tent which the mandali had put up for the meeting.

All the visitors were waiting outside the tent, their eyes glued in the direction from which Baba would come. There was a complete silence, everyone waiting for the first glimpse of their beloved Master from whom they had for so long been separated.

Then, moving like the wind, He came towards the group, and His radiant life touched them and they all seemed revitalized and reawakened.

He went into the tent and sat on His *gardee* on a platform at one end of the tent. The floor of the platform was covered with a soft green carpet, while over the *gardee* was spread a bright yellow silk covering which had been the property of some Pope and had been brought to India by Norina. It made a suitable setting for Baba's beauty.

The guests sat on chairs facing the platform, and Baba had arranged that I should sit about halfway down the tent by the side door, facing across the room. I could therefore see Baba on my right side and the men on my left. For a short time there was silence. Some small triangular flags flapped on the tent poles, the sunshine flickered on the tent, and all eyes were fixed on the lively and loving figure of their Master from whom they had been too long parted.

After a time He started to speak on His board, each sentence being vocalized first by Donkin in English, then by three other disciples in turn, using Gujarati, Hindu and Marathi.

He spoke of the work they were doing for Him and the way they were living their lives for Him. He addressed a few of them personally, asking questions and giving them much happiness with the personal attention. They seemed hungry for Him.

After some time, He announced that He had something of importance that He would like them to do for Him.

They would each be handed a paper which would explain what He wished, and if they felt they could do it, they would sign the paper. He added that He would be sad if they felt it was impossible to do this for Him, but if they ever repeated His request to one other person His deep anger would be aroused.

The mandali then handed a paper to everyone in the tent.

One was given to me. If I felt that the women mandali would agree to Baba's request, I was to sign it.

Soon after this, the meeting broke up and Baba went away, watched by the men who, till He disappeared, were unable to take their eyes from Him.

I believe He saw them again the next day.

Baba made me tell the girls about the paper I had signed. They were quite happy about it.

Moti and Mohammed

For the first few years in India, whenever we were staying on Meherabad Hill, it was my job to look after the animals. I had to pick enormous ticks out of the dogs' ears and to exercise them, to feed the five small monkeys who lovingly tore my clothes to pieces and to look after the deer, a beautiful animal called Lily, who was somewhat of a snob, always attempting to butt the garden servants, but greeting the rest of us with much affection and grace.

But the beauty and pride of the small zoo was Moti, the peacock. Every morning as the sun came up over the horizon, Moti would come down from his perch on the top of a high swing and walk across the compound for his breakfast. But not a second before the sun appeared did he move.

He knew exactly how to show off his beauty to its greatest advantage. One day a most brilliant rainbow filled the sky. Its half circle was complete—with no weakening of the color in the center. Moti stalked out onto the field, turned around, faced those who were gazing at the rainbow and opened his tail, making a perfect center for the half circle of colored light. I have seen stage stars do a worse job for themselves.

At one time, Mohammed the mast was living in a room on the opposite side of the compound from the women's quarters, and there Baba would go and spend time with him.

One afternoon, Baba with Mohammed came into the compound. He called me and smilingly spelt out that Mohammed had taken a fancy to Moti, and that I must fetch the bird and hand him over to Mohammed. Not an easy job. Moti was some distance away across the fields taking an afternoon stroll.

Laden with some green vegetable, I went across the field and holding out pieces to the bird, enticed him slowly back to where Baba was standing with His well-loved mast. The remains of the bait were handed over to Mohammed who, smiling and pleased, walked off followed by Moti. Baba looked pleased and amused at Mohammed's childlike pleasure.

A day or so later Moti returned. Mohammed had tired of him. I was glad.

The Fatties and Daulat

I t was arranged that the wife and three daughters of Kaikobad, a disciple who after serving Baba for many years followed a different path from the rest of us and was literally able to see Baba in everything and everywhere, should come to Meherabad and be taken care of in the ashram.

They were scheduled to arrive in the early evening, and beds for the girls were prepared in a long upper room where most of the women and the servants had their sleeping quarters.

Since one of the girls was coming straight from a good boarding school, and the other two were in no way prepared for the more or less primitive life of an ashram, it was arranged to let them down lightly. We put on some reasonably presentable clothes and generally tried to raise the tone of living around the place. The newcomers failed, however, to arrive when expected, and we were told not to wait for them but to go to bed. About ten o'clock that evening they arrived, and because of the lateness of the hour they received no special welcome, but were shown straight-away to their beds.

At that time I had charge of Geisha, a handsome Siamese cat. And since she was in heat at this time, and almost every night the "bokas" (large male cats) came hopefully up from the village to prowl around outside the house, I had to keep Geisha at the foot of my bed, carefully using the mosquito net to tuck her into safety.

The newcomers were no sooner tucked up in bed than the largest boka I have ever seen arrived on the windowsill nearest to Geisha's refuge. Meowing like a steam engine, he jumped in through the window and then through the netting, causing Geisha also to scream loudly and jump off the bed through the torn net. The servants, who slept on bedding rolls on the floor, not knowing what had happened, joined in the screaming and everyone else in the two long adjoining rooms started to react noisily.

The two cats tore down the long room, followed by practically everyone else, and a noisy confusion reigned supreme. And, in the midst of all the hubbub, out of their mosquito nets peered the pale, startled faces of the newcomers.

The boka was finally driven out of the building and Geisha was safely shut into an old cage. After everything had subsided, Rano and I in our neighboring beds suddenly saw the humor of the careful let-down-lightly preparations for the girls and what actually happened, and we laughed until the tears rolled down our faces.

It was certainly a startling welcome to ashram life. These girls came to be affectionately known as the Three Fatties. No explanation needed.

Daulat

Since I was not altogether a success on the domestic side of ashram life, Baba gave me other work to do, such as looking after the animals, helping the Fatties with their English, and teaching Daulat that language from the beginning.

Daulat was the daughter of Baidul, a disciple who, because of his great gift for dealing with masts, was most useful to Baba. His wife, two daughters and a son were living on a farm in Persia, and Baba had Baidul send for them to come to India. The wife and daughters came to the ashram, and the boy went to an uncle in Bombay.

I believe that if a disciple has made karmic ties, such as marriage and children, the Master takes this piece of karma on Himself and looks after the physical needs of the family. Daulat, although a most ignorant young girl, had a wonderful ear for languages, and was chatting away in Gujarati or Marathi before the Westerners could use either language to ask for a cup of tea.

Among the short poems and nursery rhymes that I used to help train Daulat's quick ear in her English studies was, "Baa, baa, black sheep, have you any wool?" which she would recite with great earnestness.

Years later, after she had married and was living in Bombay, Baba one day went to her home and met her children.

She proudly told her small boy to recite Baba's special piece of poetry. The child looked at Baba and, to His amusement, dramatically recited, "Ba-ba black sheep, have you any wool?"

Rishi Kesh

Baba and His disciples were staying in Dehra Dun when He announced that He was going to Rishi Kesh to stay for about a month and was taking them all with Him. This extraordinary place is the home of yogis, rishis and sannyasins—in fact, spiritual aspirants of all kinds.

It spreads along the banks of the Ganges, starting just where the river rushes swiftly out of the Himalayan foothills. The river carried log rafts guided by wild-looking men who stood on these contraptions, using large paddles to steer them to towns and villages far down the river towards the sea. The place was surrounded by hills which held the intense heat immobile, making it perhaps the hottest place we were ever in. Some of us, I remember, on bad days would not venture out without a damp towel worn under a solar topi.

To get to this place from Dehra Dun—which was not too far away—we had to motor through a forest. At that time I was taking care of Irene who was suffering from catatonic seizures and one never knew when she would grunt and go off into a trance. She would be unable to move, but could hear everything that went on around her. I was not allowed to give her amyl nitrate until four hours after she had passed out. Up to that time, I was supposed to pinch her fingers and toes and use hot water bottles to try and draw the blood back to the extremities. Baba, therefore, sent Irene and me, accompanied by Nilu and another sick person, in a separate car; the others as usual went in the bus.

We reached the bank of the Ganges without Irene having an attack and, meeting Baba and the rest of the party, got on board a most strange-looking boat. It was rather like an enormous Venetian gondola, with at least a dozen wild-looking tribesmen wielding paddles with which they foiled the rushing Ganges, preventing our being swept miles down the river. And then, just about halfway across the river, Irene gave her familiar grunt, passed out and fell across my knees. Baba looked at me reproachfully and, on reaching the other bank, signed to me to remain where I was and help would be sent. Everyone else went along the river path to the house.

So there we were, left in a wild place surrounded by wild-looking men, unable to move; and since Irene was still lying across my knees and was a big, heavy girl, I could do nothing for her. We just waited miserably in the stunning heat.

Then a miracle happened.

Along the bank came a most elegant-looking Hindu personage. He had four servants carrying a canopy to shelter him from the sun, and was dressed in elegant Hindu clothes.

Against the wild surroundings, he did not seem possible.

He stopped, looked at the boat, then said with an impeccable Oxford accent, "Can I help you ladies?"

I briefly explained the trouble.

He immediately told his servants to put down the canopy and two of them, under his directions, stepped onto the boat and in the prescribed manner immediately began to pinch Irene's fingers and toes. They were so strong and skillful that her circulation was quickly restored and she sat up, a bit dazed but moving. This gracious person then, to my surprise, asked if we were of Meher Baba's party. He seemed happy to learn that we were. Just then Dr. Nilu came along the bank with a chair for Irene and two men to carry it to the house.

I did hear afterwards that our friend met Baba and became a follower.

I hope so.

The house which had been lent to Baba was a large one situated very low in the valley, which kept the heat heavy around us. It was close to the Forest of Austerities where many of the sannyasins slept in concrete huts on concrete beds with concrete pillows. There were also numbers of the largest scorpions I have ever seen to keep them company. These sannyasins, who had fulfilled all their worldly duties, seen their wives comfortably settled—a must, I believe, before leaving the world—wandered over the hills dressed in saffron-colored garments, meditating, walking, and at intervals saying "Aum." Every morning at sunrise they dipped themselves in the Ganges, each time calling out "Aum." One day just before sunset—it was too hot earlier in the day—all Baba's women disciples went to the edge of the Ganges, about a hundred yards from the house, to wash their clothes in the icy waters and then spread them on the rocks, where they dried in about ten minutes.

On this particular day, we had a delightful surprise. While we were waiting for the clothes to dry, Baba unexpectedly came from the house to join us. He indicated that we should sit with Him on the sand, making a large circle. It was one of those particularly lovely moments with Baba.

There was no talking. Just the serene sky illumined by the sinking sun, the rushing Ganges swirling past, making its own music, and all of us sharing Baba's silence of Love.

After a short time, two sannyasins came in sight, saw the group and walked towards us.

They did not see Baba. We were all in light or white clothing, as He was. It was a large circle and I do not think they expected to find Baba there.

They addressed the circle at large, asking if there was any way of getting a glimpse of Meher Baba.

Everyone was silent.

Baba then told Mani to point Him out to them. It was very touching. They immediately went down on their knees, bent forward and put their foreheads on the ground. They remained there for about two minutes and then rose, seemingly perfectly contented, and, asking for nothing else, saluted Baba, turned and went slowly away.

To see these ardent seekers content with so little brought a sweeping realization of how much we were being given. Strangely, one felt humble and as if tears were very near the surface.

A few days later two more of these men bravely knocked on the gate of a walled yard where Baba spent time with the men. When the gate was opened by one of Baba's men, they asked if it were possible to see Meher Baba. Baba was sitting just inside the gate. They did not recognize Him and, since Baba did not indicate His wishes, no one pointed Him out. The men waited a moment, then turned and went away.

They did not seem to have such fortunate karma as

the first pair, but at least they came close to the Master.

A short distance up the river was a beautiful hanging bridge, leading almost to the uphill road which went to Badri, where Krishna is supposed to have said goodbye to certain disciples before leaving them and this world.

One day one of Baba's disciples was walking towards this bridge to meet Baba who had been, I believe, on a mast trip. The road leading to the bridge passed through part of the Forest of Austerities, and the disciple on his way through noticed someone in one of the stone huts.

He looked in and found to his surprise a young boy of about fourteen who said that he had left his home and was going up into the Himalayas to find a spiritual master, and that he had heard there was a great master staying in this particular neighborhood. He was hoping to catch a glimpse of Him. The disciple said nothing about Baba to the boy, but went on to meet Baba and, as they were walking back, told him about the boy. At once Baba insisted on going to the hut and signed to the disciple to ask the boy to tell his story again.

The boy did so, and then Baba told him who He was, and said that He Himself would be the boy's master—on four conditions:

1. That the boy should always beg for his food.
2. He was never to touch a woman.
3. He was never to touch money.
4. He would never in this life see Baba again.

The boy bravely accepted these formidable conditions. Baba then returned to the house and sent the boy a bag of flour and a photo of Himself. I never heard what happened to this boy, but a few days later Irene and I did meet him down by the river. He was a handsome child, and my mind kept wondering about the chances of a boy of the Western world loving God so much that he would leave home and suffer physical hardships in the hope of coming closer to Him. What with television, psychiatrists and other anomalous advantages of the present era, a search sacrificing everything in the hope of finding God, I felt, would be more likely to show up later in life.

Sometimes in the evening Baba would call us to sit with Him on a flat expanse of roof where, even though it was after dark, it was so hot that we found it difficult to sit down. This particular spot held the heat to an unimaginable extent.

One evening Baba told me to find a story and read it aloud to the party. And so, by the light of a lantern which at intervals gave forth popping sounds, I read the only story I could find at such short notice. Luckily it was a strange story and fitted in quite well with our more than strange surroundings: a dark sky, the noise of the Ganges, the heat of the roof itself and the popping lantern. Yes, *Rip Van Winkle*, Washington Irving's masterpiece, even though a New England story, strangely fitted in, did its work well to entertain, enhanced the strange atmosphere and, more than anything else, gave pleasure to Baba.

About a year before we had this longish stay in Rishi Kesh, Baba had motored us there to spend a day. He took us to a bank of the Ganges at some distance from the house about which I have been writing and showed us two interesting phenomena.

On a piece of slightly raised ground were seated a few yogis, who had gone a long way along their chosen path and had reached a stage where they seemed to be in bliss. Like the figurines of bodhisattvas in the Metropolitan Museum of Art in New York, the corners of their lips and eyes were turned up, their skin was of a beautiful dark cream color and they sat cross-legged with closed eyes, oblivious to everything but the state of spiritual bliss that they must have worked for through many incarnations. Behind each one was a small, pointed straw hut. I gathered that the nearby villagers saw to their food, etc. I think Baba saw that we were all very impressed, and that perhaps one or two were wondering if they would ever get to that state.

He then explained to us on the alphabet board that their state was not the end of the long journey to union with God, but that to reach that state they would have to reincarnate, perhaps many times, and go through the world to find God. One cannot bypass the world to get to God.

We immediately realized that we did not need bliss. We had Baba's Love. Emerson seemed to have something when he touched his poem "Brahma" with the line: "And thou meek lover of the good find Me and turn your back on heaven."

Another extremely interesting and puzzling sight was that of a yogi whose master had given him orders to stand stark naked on the bank of the Ganges and, from dawn to sunset, watch the passage of the sun across the sky. He was not to take his eyes off the ball of light until it sank below the horizon. He was a large man and appeared strong and healthy. It seemed extraordinary that his eyes could stand such treatment, especially with the fierceness of the sun's rays in that part of India.

The Mad Dog Story

After a good hot summer in Meherabad, Baba announced that He was going to move all of us to Lahore. Since we were, on the whole, quite ignorant about where or when it was hottest in India, it seemed if we were going north that it might be cooler. Our mistake. We arrived for the beginning of the Lahore summer with temperatures sometimes 115° day and night!

Baba, by this time, had stopped coddling His Western disciples. We seemed to have come to the state that one reads about in relation to following a spiritual teacher. Not quite as far down as we went later on, but certainly very difficult. For instance, about half the disciples were housed separately in a place quite near to where Baba was living and were told that for the two months in Lahore they would not see Baba. Not even once. Kitty, Rano and I were in the same house with Baba and the girls.

The two houses were quite isolated from the neighboring village and were situated about seven miles from Lahore.

They were also close to a large field where dozens of repulsive-looking vultures waited on trees and fences for the peasants to bring and abandon their dying cattle, and as soon as, but not before, the animals died these unpleasant birds flapped down from their perches for a good meal.

In most of the places where we had spent time with Baba, we had been allowed to feed the half-starved pariah dogs. They were usually animals abandoned by soldiers when their regiment moved on to another place. When we arrived in Lahore, Baba announced that in Lahore He did not wish us to do this. There was, however, a large black dog already hanging about the place and, to everyone's surprise, Mehera who rarely asked for things asked if this particular animal might be fed. Since Baba did not refuse any request made by Mehera, He spelt out on the board that the dog might be fed but that Margaret must first give the animal a bath. I felt a little apprehensive about bathing a half-starved dog and asked if I might first of all give him a meal or two just to let him know I was a friend. Well, this all went through successfully and the next move in this affair was Baba calling me into His room and telling me He was going off on a mast hunt and would I do something for Him. This was unusual. He always said do this or do that. Of course I said that I would do what He asked. Then, He said that while He was away He would like me to obey Mehera in anything she might ask me to do. We all, of course, did what we could to please Mehera, but the idea of obedience was not there. I was puzzled but happy to do what Baba wished.

A few days after Baba's departure, Mehera sent for me and asked me to bathe another dog which had come prowling around hoping for a few tidbits of food. This was a small brown dog. I bathed him and at the side of his neck found a strange gouged-out hole into which I put some ointment. The dog was given a meal and then went back to the neighboring village.

One morning after Baba's return, we were all

gathered on the front porch with Him when the brown dog made a return visit. This time he was a different animal. His eyes seemed crossed, his knees almost knocked together and he moved slowly. At once, Baba said, "That dog is mad. One of you must put a rope on him and take him to the gate. Give him to Dr. Nilu who will take him to a veterinarian." No one offered to do this.

Baba then said, "If no one will, then Margaret must."

As you can imagine, I did not feel elated about this; but since obedience had become more or less a habit, I covered my arms, borrowed some gloves, put a rope round the dog's neck and took him to the gate where Nilu, who had been sent for, was waiting. A vet to whom he was taken refused to accept him. I believe he was taken to the river and drowned.

Now no one had noticed that the original black dog who had remained with us had been behaving peculiarly. He had been hiding behind things, trying to get into the shade, his knees had dropped together, his eyes seemed strange and, mainly because we knew so little about hydrophobia, no one took any notice.

Sometimes just before going to bed, Baba would sit with us on the front porch. One peaceful evening when the party broke up He came towards me, gave me an embrace and said, "Now I am going to make you happy."

The next afternoon, Kitty called me and asked me to take the newspaper to the other house where half the party was staying. She also asked me to give a bowl of milk and water to the black dog who was lying just outside our front gate.

Directly the animal's eyes fell on the liquid, his lethargy disappeared. He jumped up in the air, then made straight for me, bit me on the right wrist and on the right knee. I fought him off with the newspaper, and when the paroxysm was over he lay down as if exhausted.

I turned and went back up to the house where I met Baba and the girls. They were sympathetic but not unduly so. Nilu was sent for but to my surprise and horror did not mention injections; and even though all agreed that the dog was certainly mad, nothing was done except by Mehera who gave me some ointment to stop the bleeding.

This next part of the story still seems almost unbelievable to me, but it happened. That evening after I had gone to bed Baba, Nilu and, I think, Ramjoo came and sat on the windowsill of my room while Nilu read aloud from a medical book all that it said about hydrophobia! After they had gone, I was so exhausted and unbelieving of these strange happenings that, thank goodness, I went to sleep.

The next morning I awoke to find that the glands in my neck, in the armpits and the groin were considerably swollen and there was a burning sensation in the esophagus.

Baba sent for me, looked at me lovingly and searchingly and said, "I hear that you are not feeling very well." In reply I murmured that I did not feel very well.

He then smiled lovingly and said, "I have arranged for you to have some jam for breakfast." Not having had any jam for a year or two, I ought to have felt delighted. I was, however, unmoved by the idea of jam and barely muttered a polite "thank you."

"And to help you get better, before going to bed you must take two Carter's Little Liver Pills!"

By this time, a kind of unbelief that this was happening had put me into something like a mental coma. No help anywhere. Later on, Nilu came to see me. I told him, as my doctor, about the swollen glands and he said I was a hypochondriac! He came to see me several times during the day, each time repeating the hypochondriac theme.

This ghastly situation came to an end the next day when Baba announced that Nilu would take me to the Lahore hospital where I should receive the appropriate injections.

Nilu, Kitty and I bumped in a tonga the seven miles to Lahore, where an irate pathologist made a few cutting remarks about my not coming for the injections at once.

He had with him four of Baba's men disciples who had just told him all about Baba and who gathered round to watch me get the first of a series of fourteen injections. These were given in the abdomen.

He then announced that, since he lived in our neighborhood, he would come to the house every morning to give me the other thirteen. He came every morning. The injections were given on the porch and everyone who had nothing to do came to watch!

He met Baba, fell for Him and afterwards became a close devotee.

This, of course, was the time that Baba chose for me to teach Mehera and Mani to swim.

We went to a Mohammedan girls' boarding school which had an adequate pool. The students were in purdah and therefore it was possible for Mehera to go and swim and not be seen by any men.

I was not too happy about going into the water. It is that element that sometimes brings on attacks of madness, and since I had not received the injections at once, the danger period for me was supposed to last six months.

One day Baba announced that He had arranged for a bus to take us to the Lahore Zoo and the Parsi burial ground.

I was feeling ill and thought longingly of an afternoon on my bed. The very idea of that kind of trip in the Lahore temperature was not appealing, and these places were some distance apart. I pondered. Had I the courage to ask Baba if I might stay in the house? I found I had and went to Him with the request. He looked at me as if I had hurt Him and said, "And I have arranged a treat for you." Well, there was nothing to do but go. By the time we reached the burial ground, I was convinced that I should probably stay there.

In spite of all these miseries, this dog bite in the end turned out to be a blessing. Baba announced firmly that since I should be in danger for six months I must go with Him and the girls wherever they went. So, instead of being left behind at Meherabad with the group when Baba and the girls went off somewhere, I went too. Blessings on the black dog.

After Lahore, the whole group went back to Meherabad and, after a short stay there, Baba said that He was going to Aurangabad to stay for a time. The girls were to go with Him and, because of the dog bite, I was to go with them.

We stayed in a small Moslem-type house built

round a courtyard. Owing to a shortage of water, everything in the small garden in front of the house was dying or dead.

My job was to sit on the verandah and see that no one came into the garden who should not do so. Baba's uncle, a dear old man who cried whenever he looked at Baba, guarded the gate on the outside. Someone gave me a packet of zinnia seeds. I planted them in a flower pot and shared my drinking water with them. They were growing up nicely when one day Baba's uncle fell asleep and some goats, seeing a chance, came into the garden and ate my zinnias! The only flowers for miles around. I cried, Baba's uncle cried and Baba came along and comforted both of us. He made us laugh at our silliness.

One day Baba took us to the famous Ellora Caves. It was a happy expedition, for as well as seeing these famous and wonderful caves with Baba, a touching incident occurred.

An old thin man acted as our guide through one of the caves where there were statues and reliefs of the Hindu incarnations and gods.

This man loved his gods so much that at moments there were tears in his eyes as he explained them to us.

After he had taken us round the cave, Baba signed to Mani to tell him that He, Baba, was one of the incarnations. Mani did so and the man took one look at Baba, accepted Him as such, fell on his knees and sobbed as if all his dreams of the great gods were being fulfilled, which of course they were.

For us, the disciples, it was wonderfully moving, and our sympathetic tears welled up to the surface. So much sudden love did Baba sometimes release when someone was ready for this experience.

From Aurangabad, Baba took us on another expedition. This time we went to Daulatabad, which was to be the scene of a Moslem religious ceremony. We motored through a sandy desert covered with enormous ant hills and arrived at a place in the hills where there were two mosques, a *dak* bungalow and not much else. The bungalow was being used by some British official, but when he heard it was needed by Baba's party, he politely went away, giving Baba the bungalow.

It seemed the most unlikely place in the world for a ceremony. No people in sight, no hotel, no houses.

The next day, however, was a different matter. In the night some hundreds of covered carts had arrived and had been lined up to form streets. Some serving food and selling other necessities. The hillsides were covered with men and women. Such a change was almost unbelievable.

The two mosques were about a mile apart, and the ceremony was to consist of the bones of some Moslem saint being carried from one mosque and established in the other.

The interesting thing was that the persons in charge seemed to know about Baba, and with Him, we were all allowed to enter the mosques where the saint's bones were. I suppose I was the only English person in the neighborhood. I pulled my hat down over my ears and got behind the girls when we entered the mosque. One hears about white persons having their ears chopped off or other choice things done to them if they enter a mosque uninvited. I was, however, unnoticed.

These people made a fuss about Baba. He looked happy and elated, as He often did when working on something special.

For the ceremony itself, Baba managed these people so wonderfully that we were allowed to sit in one of the alcoves on the outside of the mosque into which the bones would be carried. The alcove was just above the doorway, so that we should see the casket carried into its new home. Also we could see up the sloping road as far as the other mosque.

The ceremony was unbelievable.

First the colors. In each costume for women there were at least three colors. Usually bright green, vivid red and a darkish bright blue. Multiply this by hundreds of people milling around. In such colors, the intensity and wildness of these people pushing, screaming and trying to get near enough to the casket to touch it as it was carried down the hill has given me some idea of things that go on in the Middle East in the name of Allah. These people did not seem to be human beings, but just fanatics. The British government had sensibly sent soldiers to line each side of the route between the two mosques, and at intervals they fired their rifles into the air. This, although it gave the bones more safety, certainly added to the noisy, colorful confusion. Finally a few really wild persons broke through the cordon and nearly upset the casket containing the bones. It was rescued, however, and finally was safely carried into the mosque through the door that lay just below our feet. In the meantime, Baba had left us alone. He had apparently spotted a mast in the crowd. After a time He returned, but we still had to wait quite a long time before leaving. The crowds seemed unable to come out of this unnatural state of emotion.

If I had not seen it, I could never have imagined

that so much red-hot religious fanaticism could pour out from the core of human beings.

In the evening we went to a performance given by the traveling circus that had arrived for the festivities.

Baba was beautiful, entering into the spirit of these poor people's enjoyment. They were rather mangy lions, not very good acrobats, and the lighting was bad, but Baba sat and beamed at the whole thing. I am sure His radiant personality helped these men and women to enjoy the performance.

There was one unforgettable performance. After the regular show, as we went out of the tent into the moonlight, we found an elephant all by himself once more going through his performance. He was charming and most professional. Baba was delighted and amused by him, and stayed watching until he had finished his act.

The next day everything broke up. The covered carts departed and Baba took us back to Aurangabad.

Meherazad

After being sent by Baba for a short interval to Meherabad, I again left the group and joined Baba and the "girls" (Mehera, Mani, Nagoo, Naja, etc., were always known as the girls, and that is the word I still naturally use for them) at Meherazad.

One of my jobs was to guard the well which was outside the compound. It contained our drinking water, and the local shepherds would come down from the hills for a drink. Unfortunately, they were quite likely to put their feet in the water! So every morning I sat armed with a lathi under a tree near the well, and when these men appeared, I gave them a drink from a chatti.

It was so hot that every afternoon I developed a fever. Then I remembered an old wives' cure. Every morning I bound a large onion onto my waist, and sure enough it worked. In the afternoon the fever broke into a profuse sweat all over my body.

Sometimes just before sunset, Baba would take us for a stroll on the hills and we collected large stones that looked like glass. Mehera, who was trying to get the garden round the house into some kind of order, would use them to outline her small flower beds. At that time of the war, it was difficult to get plants as she wanted to, and these stones gave a delightful effect.

Baba seemed occasionally to enjoy a little slap-stick humor. The women's toilet at Meherabad looked like an old fashioned bathing machine on wheels. The kind that

Victorian ladies would enter a short distance away from the sea to get into a bathing suit which covered them from neck to foot. The structures would then be pulled down to the sea, so the ladies could come out, modestly unseen, and dip up and down in the water. Well, this affair was tethered in place by long ropes, one fastened to each corner and then tied to stakes driven into the ground some distance away. Early one morning, I was cleaning my teeth just near this affair—really more watching the sun come up than noticing what I was doing—and in order to see the sun more clearly, I took a step backwards, caught my foot in one of the tethering ropes and fell down backwards with a wallop.

Baba, so the girls afterward told me, was just coming out of the back door, and on seeing my ignominious performance, went straight back into the house and laughed and laughed with the greatest enjoyment. I am sorry that I was not there to laugh with Him. Laughter with Baba always seemed to be such a cleansing experience. Laughter was, and still is, a help with the "Don't worry" order.

It was in Meherazad that an unexplainable incident occurred. Someone sent Baba a beautiful Siamese cat. The animal had had a strange upbringing. It lived in a three-room cage. A place to eat, a place to sleep and a place for toilet purposes, and she did not want to come out and face the world. Baba had the cage brought to my small room—it practically filled the floor space—with orders to me to train the cat to come out and run around in the usual way of cats. It took me some weeks, but in the end "Geisha," as she had been named, would let me take her out on the hills and from there she would return alone to her room.

One evening—the first night of the monsoon—
the skies seemed to open and release something like
Niagara Falls onto Meherazad and the country round
about. It was difficult to hear anything else. Early in
the evening, Baba opened the door of my room, came in
and made signs that I should put the cat outside in the
yard. It was seldom—after all Baba's training—that I
made any protests; but this time I pointed out to Baba
that it would be hard on the animal to throw it out on
such a night. Baba gave in to me. The next evening,
however, the same thing occurred. Again I started to
argue. This time, however, Baba, who had never shown
me power, only love, seemed to shoot up to about seven
feet high, sending a wave of power towards me, and
spelt on the board, "Is this my cat or yours?" I could only
say, "Yours, Baba," and hurriedly seizing the cat, took
it to the door and threw it out into a dark bath of
descending water. Cat lovers may be pleased to hear
that Geisha found a hole in the kitchen wall and spent a
comfortable night out of the deluge.

Now this happened to be about the time during
World War II when Churchill ordered the British fleet
to cross the English channel to France. His admirals
refused to go on the grounds that bad weather rendered
a successful crossing and invasion impossible. The next
night the same thing happened, but this time Churchill
insisted that they go, which they did, and the successful
invasion of France started from that time.

If you wish to connect these incidents do so; I don't
know.

Dal and Sandals

While staying at Meherazad with Baba and the girls, I was given the privilege of eating meals with them. This was not in any way usual, and I was most happy to sit on the bottom step of the verandah and enjoy being with Baba.

One day at the midday meal I took the first spoonful of my dal and rice and found to my pleased surprise that at last my palate had changed, and that I could really appreciate this staple Indian food. How wrong I had been about this dish. It was really delicious.

After a few minutes of eating and appreciating, there seemed to be a troubled confusion at the top of the steps, and then suddenly everyone was looking down the steps at me. To my horror it was announced that I had been given the wrong dish and what I was enjoying was Baba's lunch which had been prepared for Him by Mehera's loving hands.

I do not think that during my whole life I had felt such a cloud of miserable embarrassment as at that moment. Baba's lunch! What would He eat? It was like being in the Black Hole of Calcutta. As usual, Baba saved the situation with a touch of humor. He looked sad, and intimated that His disciples seemed to be taking advantage of Him. Only that morning, He said, Chanji, who was being sent to New Delhi on a special errand, had packed and taken His most comfortable sandals with him. And now Margaret had eaten His lunch.

At this point someone rushed in from the kitchen with the news that there was plenty more of Baba's special meal, and this news was followed by the dal itself. Baba smiled happily at me, I recovered my poise and finished my ill-gotten meal, which I still feel was the most delicious that I had eaten since arriving in India.

Secunderabad

A short time later Baba went to Secunderabad. He took the girls, and I went with them.

We started in a smallish house on the edge of a sandy desert. Every night one of the rooms of the house filled up with snakes. They were lovely to watch. They danced and circled and were the epitome of graceful movement. The door of this room was closed at night. In spite of that, I very firmly tucked in my mosquito curtains, and I think the others also took this safety measure.

It was in this house that Mehera asked Baba if I could read English poetry with her. We both loved poetry, and in my bedding roll I had a copy of the *Oxford Book of Verse*. So, with Baba's approval, we spent an hour or two every day finding out Mehera's tastes. She was most drawn to the romantics, Keats and Shelley, but was not drawn to anything modern. I think we both enjoyed this sharing of something we each loved.

Secunderabad, which is a suburb of Hyderabad, was chiefly inhabited by a great many English army people. Every morning, I had to take Mani's dog for a walk. It was a treat to go out alone, but the appearance of an English woman unknown in the social circles of the suburb aroused curiosity.

One morning, a most personable young man galloped up to me, reined in his horse and said, "Didn't I see you at Lady so-and-so's party the other evening?"

Since I knew that Baba would not wish me to say what I was doing there, I looked at him firmly and said curtly, "No, you did not," and stalked on with my mongrel dog and my ashram clothes.

A few days later, however, a woman opened a window as I was passing her house, and made a similar kind of opening, which I again had to squash.

After a few days in the snaky house, we moved to a beautiful house with a swimming pool and every Indian luxury.

This house had just been built by a wealthy Hindu lawyer for himself and his family.

While this house was being built, a wandering holy man came along the road, took one look at the house, sat down crosslegged on the other side of the road, and went into a deep meditation. When he came back from this state, he told the builders that the greatest spiritual entity in the world would be the first person to live in this house. The lawyer, who happened to be there, laughed and said that he himself was going to move in at once. Little did he know about Baba! Baba sent Donkin along to this man, saying that He would like to live there for a short time, and with Baba at the back of him, Donkin persuaded this man to let Baba have His way.

So we left the snakes, the sand and the dirt to the men disciples, and moved into this house.

The house had everything, even a spacious swimming bath, and there Mehera and Mani continued their swimming lessons.

In my life, I have done a great deal of teaching, but never before or since have I taught anyone with a one-pointed mind. Mehera's mind was one-pointed to Baba, and when Baba told her to learn to swim, she turned this one-pointedness at His wish onto learning to swim. It was a miracle. At once, she was able to do what I said and did not forget anything. She was strong physically, and during the two months we were in Secunderabad, she could use skillfully four different strokes, could swim a length under water, and dive beautifully and cleanly.

We were joined by Rano Gayley, and she and I shared a room. Although Rano and I had a real affection for each other, at the slightest provocation we would become involved in an argument about something not worth arguing about. This sometimes led to us both shouting at each other and being most unpleasant. Even though Baba had threatened us with dire consequences and we really tried to stop it, it still at intervals rushed up to the surface.

One hot evening at bedtime, I went into the bedroom and found an enormous green lizard, about a foot long, crawling around the wall near the ceiling. Since these creatures sometimes had poisonous droppings, I fetched a long broom and propelled it along towards an outlet. I naturally felt that we might sleep better without its presence. I was getting along nicely when in came Rano who at once objected to the way I was doing this. Up came a storm. We said the most cutting and unkind things to each other, and then found that our Master was standing in the doorway looking sternly at us.

He called us out onto a balcony, sent for the girls, and we sat down in a kind of semi-circle, with Rano and I looking like prisoners at the bar. Baba spelt on the board, and Mani translated, that if Rano and I did not behave we should be sent away. There was also quite a long dissertation on our characters, and after a time I really broke, and sobbed out that I had for some years tried to surmount this situation and that I was not going to try anymore. Boo-hoo!

Strange as it may seem, from that time the situation slowly got better, and now Rano and I have a great affection and friendship for each other.

It seems to me that Baba would bring a small portion of the ego up to the surface, and then find suitable means to batter the ugly thing away. It takes a long time. Four to five years for Rano and I to clear that small piece away.

Rano was having some trouble with her teeth. She was given permission to go into Hyderabad to visit a dentist, and Donkin was told to escort her in a tonga and see that all was well. She returned elated, came to our room and gave me a small packet of English toffee as a present from Donkin. Since I had never cared for Indian sweets, this was most acceptable; but it was not to be. On turning round, we found Baba in the doorway, watching the whole transaction. He signed to Rano to take the toffee, go across an unpleasant, sandy, snake-ridden piece of ground and return the packet to Donkin at the men's house.

There was plenty of time in Secunderabad to sit round Baba in the evenings, and my job was to read aloud from Agatha Christie and other good stories of the kind that Baba seemed to enjoy so much. Usually, as the story was working up, and the next chapter would certainly produce the crisis that would tell us who-done-it, Baba would smile and send us all off to bed, leaving the mystery unsolved. I, who had charge of the books, was forbidden to peep ahead and satisfy my curiosity.

Near the end of the stay in Secunderabad, we had a strange week.

Baba announced that for one week He was going to fast. He gave Mehera permission to fast with Him for one day.

No newspapers came to the house. One day after the midday meal, at the hottest hour of the Indian day when everyone usually had a nap, Baba sent for me. He was alone and sent me to fetch a book and read out loud to Him. I found a book and when I returned, He indicated where I should sit to read. He lay down on His bed and covered Himself from head to foot with a sheet. It was like reading to a mummy. The midday heat was intense and Baba had mysteriously disappeared under a cover. My voice echoed strangely round the empty room and finally, when I felt my senses had almost disappeared and I might perhaps faint, Baba suddenly sprang right up from the bed and sent me away. This curious and unnerving experience was repeated at the same time on the following day.

Two days after this, I was taking Mani's dog for a stroll when I observed a large house that had been decorated with flags. Curiosity took me across the road to the house, and I found the name on the gate was Lieutenant-Colonel so-and-so. We, the women disciples, for the past few days had seen no newspapers and heard no news, but those waving flags on an army officers' house could mean only one thing. The Second World War was over. This was so.

Bubonic Plague

After spending some little time at Meherazad, Baba took the party to Ahmednagar to stay in a house lent Him by Katie's father. It was situated very near the bazaar where one day we heard that bubonic plague had broken out.

The British, who at that time were all powerful in Ahmednagar, ordered inoculations against this terrible disease for everyone in the neighborhood. Unwilling peasants were pulled from buses, homes were entered, cabs were stopped; in fact, no one could escape.

Except Baba and His group.

Sarosh, who was the mayor of Ahmednagar, was told by Baba, "No inoculations for any of us." He was devastated. I think he saw, and probably he was right, that if it leaked out that we had had no treatments, his whole successful business career would be finished. The army would not forgive. Up to the time Baba gave this order, I think that we had been alarmed. I know I was. So easy. Just a flea from a dead rat in the market, a small unnoticed bite, and then agony. Directly Baba said, "No injections," the fear went completely and did not return.

I think Sarosh was the one who suffered most. He had to drive me somewhere. He was white and nervous and said quite violently, "You are all leaving here next week and am I thankful!"

Baba went away for a day or two to see a mast, and

my orders were to go round the garden every day, and if I saw a dead rat, we were to jump into the bus, not to pack, and go at once to Meherabad. There were no rats, and after Baba's return we all went back to Meherabad.

Judas Iscariot and Hitler

wo short stories in which Baba showed us the
spiritual meaning of certain events to which we
had shown the ordinary worldly attitudes.

Judas Iscariot

Sometimes in the evenings at Meherabad, Baba
would sit on his *gardee* and the women of the ashram,
plus the servants, would bring their personal straw mat
and sit cross-legged on the ground around Him. A few
sat on chairs. Mehera always had a chair on Baba's
right side, and one or two of the older disciples, whose
knees were no longer supple enough for the floor
position, would use chairs.

The gatherings were usually quite informal and
Baba encouraged us to bring up subjects, give opinions,
and then sometimes would show us that, although we
might be thinking along the right lines from a worldly
point of view, from the spiritual angle we were quite
wrong.

One evening the subject of Judas Iscariot's betrayal
of Jesus came up for discussion and, looking at beloved
Baba, our minds at once made the connection between
Him and Jesus, and a certain amount of hostility was
shown towards Judas, whose very name has come to
mean "traitor." After a short time, Baba stopped this
and explained that Judas was of Jesus's circle, and
since the betrayal was a necessary prelude to the

crucifixion, someone had to do it. Judas had been chosen and, blindfolded, he had served his Master.

After we had digested this, Baba added that Judas was again in incarnation and working in the Circle; and then, seeing our eyes shift uneasily from one to another, hoping not to be the one, He smilingly reassured the group that the reincarnated Judas was not present with us on this occasion.

Although we did realize the amazing service that Judas had done for Jesus, it was a relief to feel that one of us in an earlier life had not been called upon to serve our Master in this manner.

Hitler

Baba was the first of the Avatars to travel around the world, unhampered by the lack of speedy travel facilities which had confined Krishna, Buddha and Jesus to small portions of the globe, from where the knowledge of them and their teachings had spread slowly outwards. Before World War II, Baba had already traveled to many countries and continents, and He called these many contacts, both personal and geographic, "laying cables." Later, when necessary, He would recontact these spots—perhaps by a seemingly accidental visit by a disciple, or perhaps giving a direct order that someone should go to a certain place. Even a letter or cable would sometimes do the job.

Although Baba Himself never went into Germany, He did send certain disciples who had social or business connections into the country to talk of Him. Just a few days before Hitler's big coup in Munich, a close disciple had been in the city.

It seems that since every personal ego has to come up to the surface and function before it can be destroyed, so the national ego, the religious ego, etc., must undergo in the same way the same process of destruction. Love can then flow in to replace them. After the war Baba told us this cleansing had by no means been fully accomplished, and that there was a choice of two ways to accomplish the rest.

One would be a third and devastating world war, and the other way would be through small wars, earthquakes, general physical upheaval, starvation for some groups, and religious groups vying with each other, their adherents killing each other to prove that their way was the only way to God.

Baba then looked around the group and asked which we thought was the better way. For once unanimous, we said, "The second way." He made no indications as to the direction in which humanity would be swept, but certainly most of the things that He mentioned as the second way have already happened and are still, in many parts of the world, continuing to cause a general upheaval.

Baba told us when our tongues were making an outraged attack on Hitler and his cruelties that again we did not understand, but that when He, the Avatar, comes into incarnation He needs opposition in order to function fully.

An Impression

At the foot of Meherabad Hill between the railway line and the men's quarters lies a grave.

One morning some of the women living at that time on the hill were called down to watch the ceremony that Baba was conducting in memory of certain close disciples who had died some distance from the ashram of their beloved Master.

Baba was radiant. He was illuminated by a cloud of joy and love for these men who had served Him lovingly and faithfully.

It was a wide-open grave and as the name of each of these disciples was called He threw into the grave some object representing the named disciple. A rose for one, a suit of clothes for another, and some sandals for another. This beautiful ceremony swept away the conventional sadness of death, making it simply another and continuing part of life.

Baba then walked across the road to a platform which had been erected especially for the occasion, and sat there in the middle of a half-circle made by the closest and strongest male disciples. He then gave a short talk. Somehow I did not give full attention to what Baba was saying. Instead I seemed to be obsessed by and drowning in a feeling that nothing destructive could happen to a world in which Baba and such a strong circle existed; that nothing of evil could possibly penetrate such a barrier. It looked impenetrable.

God Is Love

Towards the end of my stay in India, for those under Baba's loving but severe discipline everything went down to a very low living level.

One summer at Meherabad, Baba having disappeared—most probably to visit some newly discovered mast—it seemed that we had come close to experiencing life at a poor Indian peasant level. The servants would collect cow dung, water it down to a very liquid consistency and joyfully, since it was like home, spread it thickly over the compound floor, including that of our eating quarters. It was supposed to keep the dust from being blown into everything. This was probably true, but there was something worse than dust.

On hearing of the cow-dung fiesta, every fly in the neighborhood sent out messages to friends all over the country to come at once. "Come and have a lavish time." The result was horrendous. I can remember some of us trying to eat the midday meal under a large towel which covered our heads and plates.

As soon as Baba returned, the cow dung spreading came to an end. But there was a worse trial in store.

Every afternoon Baba would come up the hill from the men's quarters, join the "girls" in their room and refuse to see the rest of the group; even going as far as to arrange that none of us should even catch a glimpse of Him. As Baba left the men's quarters a bell was sounded, we crossed the compound, went into a large room and remained there until the sound of the bell again released us—usually after about two hours.

There was nothing much to do. Rano tried to get on with some painting, others mended their clothes, and a few wrote letters.

One afternoon, I put an enormous navy blue patch into the seat of my only pair of slacks, which were already covered with patches of various colors. I gazed admiringly at the result of my work. The sun was beating down on the corrugated iron roof, and somehow I felt that I should make an effort to show that I felt no ill-will towards this boring and seemingly endless situation.

Extracting some green embroidery silk from my sewing bag, I embroidered the words "God is Love" onto the patch, put on the slacks and paraded around, giving everyone the only laugh of the afternoon.

Baba, hearing about this the next afternoon, sent for me, made me stand with my back to Him, and seemed to be amused by the patch. After all, it expressed the whole truth of the universe, even if appearing in a slightly unconventional spot.

The Story of Millicent Deakes

In 1931, a woman by the name of Millicent Deakes, who was at that time living in the Andaman Islands, took a trip to India to see Baba. For some time she had been corresponding with Chanji, and then one day she decided that the time had come to see Baba. Alas! Before setting out on this trip, she did not seem to think it necessary to find out if Baba would be available or even if He would see her. Therefore, when she arrived, she found that He was away. He was taking His first trip to the West.

A few years later she tried again, and again mistimed her visit.

When the second World War reached that part of the East, she was taken prisoner and spent the rest of the war in a concentration camp at Singapore.

As soon as the war was over, the British arranged for many of their nationals to go to regain health and sanity at some of the Indian hill-stations. Millicent was among them.

After a time she found herself in Bombay, and at once the longing to see Baba reasserted itself. Again, instead of making an appointment, she arrived at Meherabad, where Baba refused to see her.

The poor woman went back to Bombay where, after a time, she received a message from Baba telling her to come to Ahmednagar, and that this time He would see her.

She spent a short time with Baba, and then He sent her to have the evening meal on the hill at the women's quarters. Since we never had visitors, the housekeeper—Katie, I think—was in a difficulty. Our enamel plates by this time had not much enamel; the mugs—also enamel—were stained by strong tea; and the knives and spoons were at about the same level. The compound where we ate was, in the evening when she came, lit by hurricane lamps, the globes of which were held together by sticking plaster and which at intervals gave out strange sounds. Everyone had her own utensils which she washed and kept in a special place on a shelf.

Millicent Deakes did not take much notice of us. She was crying and continued to do so. Her mind was completely on Baba and her interview with Him. We barely existed.

When we finally sat down to eat, she came back to the world, looked round at us and at the primitive arrangements, probably sensing a mild embarrassment on our part, then said, "Don't worry about me. I have just come from a concentration camp myself."

And just for one moment, we saw ourselves as the outside world might have seen us.

Birthday Cake

Towards the end of World War II Baba was, with the disciples, staying in Dehra Dun. On Baba's birthday, to celebrate the occasion, Katie and Kitty made a cake. At this time it was not possible to obtain all the ingredients to make a good cake, but they made up for lack of flavor-inspiration by building a magnificent cake of seven tiers. Each tier, of course, representing one of the spiritual planes.

It was round in shape and each tier, as the cake went up, was slightly smaller than the one before. A small wooden ladder ran up the side and a figure, rather shapeless, had managed to crawl up to the "third plane."

In the evening, the cake was presented, and Baba showed His loving admiration and pleasure, and everyone was happy. Baba then stepped forward, touched the cake, seized the seventh plane section, tore it off and took it out of the room. Well, that put all of us where we belonged! Baba returned, cut the rest of the cake, and then said that He would give us a little wine.

In all the years I was with Him, I do not remember this happening more than three times. We sat round the room, crosslegged on the floor, and suddenly this wine went to my head. Looking at Baba, I felt and saw that He was Easter Sunday. This may sound like nonsense, but as a child that day had always meant for me that light had come after the dark winter.

Baba then called me and I sat on the floor beside His chair, with my head on His knee. After a time He leaned down and spelled on the board: "Tonight is Heaven."

I had a moment of truth and stammered out, "Yes, but tomorrow won't be."

Baba laughed.

In America

*I am the Divine Beloved, who
loves you more than
you can ever love yourself.*

MEHER BABA

Return Journey

After seven wonderful but battering years with Baba, He told me to go back to England, and then to go on to the U.S.A. and there to teach ballet. At that time, very soon after World War II, traveling was difficult, and unless one was going to make business connections for England, it was almost impossible to get from there to America. I mentioned this to Baba and all He did was to smile—stretch out His hands and smile.

He arranged for me to leave Dehra Dun on May 1, 1946, and on that day I departed. (Usually dates were changed.) Baba, accompanied by Kaka, escorted me on the night train as far as New Delhi. It was most unusual, but I traveled in the same compartment with Him and Kaka. I was badly anemic and was suffering from an onslaught of large, painful boils, and although I lay on an uncomfortable slatted seat and, more than that, this was to be my last time for some long period with Baba, I slept in a kind of heavy exhaustion. Whenever I opened my eyes, it was to see Baba sitting up on the opposite seat, His legs crossed in the usual yoga position, apparently discussing something with Kaka; and each time He waved me back to sleep.

On our arrival at New Delhi station, Baba disappeared and Donkin appeared, to give me breakfast at the station restaurant. This was perfectly all right, but since my train south did not go till the evening, he politely invited me to luncheon at his club. I refused, and I think he was relieved. To offer to take someone whose clothes made her look like a charwoman to luncheon at an exclusive English military club was an act of great nobility. I had on an overall, a solar topi with a broken rim, no stockings and peasant sandals. My train to Ahmednagar, where I was to break my journey to Bombay, did not start until midnight, and I spent the day in a waiting room. Sometime in the afternoon, the ayah brought me a message telling me to go outside. I did so and there was Baba to say goodbye. He embraced me, made a sweeping movement with His hands up over His heart, which Kaka translated as, "Take My love to the West," and He then left me. I was left, not having been independently alone for seven years, to get myself first of all to Ahmednagar, and then to England and America.

I arrived at Ahmednagar in an exhausted condition. No one to meet me! Luckily one of Baba's local followers happened to be at the station. He was horrified to see me there alone, and took me to the men's quarters below Meherabad Hill.

Apparently the men had no idea I was coming. They were shocked and took me up the hill to Mansari, who lovingly took charge, bathed me, fed me and put me in her own bed for the night.

The next day Sarosh, who had received orders from Baba to do so, came to fetch me and drove me to Arnavaz's apartment in Bombay. Arnavaz, at Baba's express wish, housed and fed me until I departed for England. She was kindness itself.

Every one of Baba's followers that I met in Bombay was pessimistic about my chances of getting on a boat. Not for at least two months, they agreed. Then, of course, one of those seemingly impossible things happened. I went to the American Express offices, and was told there by a young man that there was no chance of getting on a boat for at least two months. After this pronouncement, he looked wistful and said, "But are you not an American?" He then told me that he was an Englishman and that he badly wanted to go back to England to have a sailing holiday on the Norfolk Broads. Again Baba's crack in the wall . . .

At once, I said, "I spent half my childhood sailing on the Norfolk Broads." We then rapturously compared notes and found that we had both been on Womack Broad, a beautiful sheet of water so difficult to find that few persons had managed to do so. He was so delighted that the next thing was, he was offering to arrange a passage for me. He said, "Be ready and packed and if anyone unexpectedly gets off a boat I will see that you get the berth. But you must be ready to go at a moment's notice."

Within ten days the call came and, accompanied by many of Baba's Bombay disciples to see me off, I went on board the ship and took the vacant berth. Baba's sense of humor again manifested strongly. Not having had much to do with men for seven years, just a slight contact with the men disciples, I now found myself on, of all places, a troop ship! There were five other women on board and we shared a cabin. When one of these importantly remarked that since her husband was a great friend of a certain maharajah, she had only had to wait two months to obtain a passage, I had to stop myself from saying, "You should know Meher Baba; it would then only have taken ten days."

My journey to India during the early part of the war had taken about six weeks. The return journey to England, on a boat carrying soldiers and important military personnel, took only ten days. After longing to see once more the green fields of England, the moment we sighted the Isle of Wight I felt as if an enormous pair of scissors was cutting my umbilical tie with the country of my birth. I did not care anymore, and the tie has never been resumed.

Delia de Leon and Will Backett met me at Waterloo Station. The latter pressed into my hand a small packet of butter. I did not, at the time, realize that it was his week's ration. Dear, kind Will.

For a few days, Minta de Leon put me up at her apartment. The morning after my arrival, I went out to see about food tickets, which were still necessary. During the walk I found that everything seemed to have changed, and as I was walking along Kensington High Street, feeling lost and inadequate, I glanced across to the other side of the busy street and there, to my amazement, in a shop window I saw Baba! Knowing that I was not of the type that has visions, I rushed across the road to find out what it was that I had mistaken for Baba, and there in a photographer's shop window was an almost life-sized enlargement of one of the photographs of Baba taken by this same photographer in 1931.

It was most comforting. I was no longer alone and lost in a changed world.

Getting to America

I t seemed as if Baba were asking for an impossibility when, about a year after the war was over, He told me that He was sending me back to the West, and that I must go to the United States and there teach ballet. I put some of the difficulties of doing this to Baba: How was I to get a job? Steamship passage to America was hard to get unless one was doing important business and making money for England.

Baba smiled happily, patted me on the back, and sent me off anyway.

As always, unexpected things completely out of my control (and only Baba could have so timed them) came into action, and within a few months I, plus job, had landed in America.

Two weeks after my landing in England, American Ballet Theatre came over to give performances. Antony Tudor, their chief choreographer, was an Englishman, a great friend of mine, who coincidentally had left England for America about the same time that I had left for India. He spoke to Lucia Chase, the director of the company, about me, and she invited me to come to America and give lessons to the company. I accepted thankfully.

The next things were visas and travel accommodations. Even after the war, when most people were shabby, I could probably have been classed as one of the seven worst-dressed women in England. Therefore, when I went to the American Embassy, a most efficient young man frankly looked me up and down and said, "Why do you want to go to America?" I explained about Ballet Theatre and I showed him my contract. His attitude immediately changed. He beamed on me, forgot my clothes, and said, "I am a balletomane. Sit down and let me see what I can do." He asked very few questions, again stated his love for ballet, and the next thing, I was walking out of the Embassy with the required papers! Since I had the papers and the contract, the steamship company made no difficulties. Baba's order was fulfilled. By New Year's Day 1947, I was teaching in San Francisco.

Naomi

aomi, on the day that I landed in America in 1946, came to the docks to greet me, and would have taken me to her home, had Elizabeth not been there with the same purpose in mind. It did, however, create for me a warm feeling about America.

She knew next to nothing about Baba, but as our acquaintanceship progressed towards friendship, she began to show interest, and this very soon changed to love for Him.

She met Him several times here in America, and went with a party of dancers to the 1962 Sahavas in Poona.

At the Sahavas, her testing time began. Up to that time, Baba had given her love and, since her sense of humor was keen, had laughed and joked with her. But now she was faced by a Baba who took very little notice of her, to the extent of hardly seeing that she was there. While she was in India, she tried to hide that anything was wrong. After that, she talked with me about it, fearful that He wanted her to leave Him. She wisely decided not to do this and hung on. Two years later, the situation was reversed and she received from Baba on her birthday a loving cablegram. The tension relaxed, and her love flowed more freely than before this difficult discipline.

A few years later, she contracted leukemia. She was at that time living in England, and although I was unable to go to see her, I heard from many friends who visited her that she had changed enormously. She wanted to talk only about Baba, and Baba's love was to be felt round her. The nearer she approached death, the more this emanation was felt by others.

Just before the end, when she was unconscious under a strong sedation, her daughter bent and whispered, "Baba," close to her ear. She seemed just for a moment to respond.

His name should be the last thing we hear, say or think.

A Difficult Journey

After a long absence, Baba in 1952 came to America again. There were a large number of persons, both young and old, who had for a long time known of Him and perhaps loved Him; and each knew that, whatever happened, they must manage to get to Myrtle Beach on the day that He had put aside to meet those anxious to make a personal contact with Him.

Among them was a group of four dancers who were attached to the Metropolitan Opera Copany: Zebra, Kathryn, Shura and Tex. The company was at this time on tour, and on the day before Baba's given day of reception would be performing in Minneapolis. The dancers found that if they could get permission from the management to go, it would be possible to fly to see Baba in Myrtle Beach, and the next day, fly to join the company in Bloomington, Indiana, in time for the evening performance. They asked several persons in the management for permission to do this. All flatly refused to help them. Finally, Rudolf Bing himself, hearing of their dilemma, generously gave the needed permission.

I cannot imagine how, out of their salaries, they managed to find the money to hire a plane, but through a friend in New York arrangements were made.

At six o'clock in the morning on the appointed day, they went to the airport and found that the weather ahead was so bad that they could not get permission to fly. The pilot, who all through this strange journey acted as if driven by some hidden force, insisted that everything was all right, and forced a grudging permission from the authorities to depart. At Chicago, there was more and worse opposition to the flight, but again this strange pilot insisted upon going on with the journey.

The same trouble faced them at Louisville. Again, however, their friend got them off the ground, but this time they were forced to return to Louisville. Finally at five o'clock, as they began to cross the mountains the weather improved, and as the sun came out they remembered that Baba had given 5 o'clock as the time when He would finish giving interviews. This was a tremendous shock. Was all this mad flight going to be for nothing?

At Myrtle Beach, however, they were met by one of Baba's mandali, who told them that Baba would see them the next morning.

The next morning they were taken to the room where He was waiting for them.

One by one, they were admitted to the presence of the one who was all Love.

One by one, He saw them and embraced them and they were enveloped in the cloud of His love.

What a worthwhile, wonderful journey!

Paul

About a year before Baba came to America in 1952, I came in contact with Paul, a young man who, from almost the first moment of his hearing about Baba, was drawn to Him by a strong love. He had no knowledge of spiritual matters, and would seem to be the most unlikely person to whom such a thing could happen. His parents had not wished ever to have a child. He was shown no love, and was often reminded that he had not been wanted. You can imagine the result of this treatment. Paul, a handsome boy with too much money, had reacted to a loveless upbringing by drinking heavily, taking drugs, and doing everything else calculated to ruin himself both physically and spiritually. By the time he heard of Baba, his face showed decided signs of dissipation.

Because of this genuine love for Baba, he made valiant efforts to curtail some of his activities and did manage for six months to keep away from alcohol.

Then Baba came to New York.

He interviewed and showed Love to many persons at Ivy Duce's home, where she had a commodious studio eminently suitable for this purpose.

Never having seen anyone of Paul's type coming to see Baba, I told Him of the boy and nervously asked if an interview were a possibility.

Baba was quite short with me and indicated that His Love was for everyone who was able to love Him, and that I should have known it.

Paul went into the room where Baba, giving out of His warmth and beauty to all those around Him, was sitting.

As this sad creature entered the room, Baba's face became irradiated with a welcoming smile of loving compassion, and His arms opened to give shelter to a sobbing Paul.

For quite a few moments he remained, crying away his sins and miseries in this sanctuary of Love.

After a little while, Baba looked at me and signalled, "He loves Me."

Baba kept Paul with Him for quite a time before sending him away.

He seemed quite different after this wonder of Love, but his wrecked, unhealthy body failed to function any longer, and soon after the meeting with Baba he died.

A strange life which, starting with no love at all, had before it ended experienced the love of Love Himself.

Myrna

Myrna was a young dancer who, almost as soon as she heard of Baba, was drawn towards Him with a strong feeling of love. Before He came to the West in 1952, she and a friend would spend evenings together, talking of Him, reading the Discourses, singing to Him, happy with the idea that He would soon come to America and that they would meet Him.

At last the news came that Baba was coming to America and would stay for a short time at the Center in Myrtle Beach, a place of great charm designed and laid out by Elizabeth and Norina, and lovingly prepared according to Baba's wishes for His long-awaited coming. Unfortunately, the man to whom Myrna was engaged to be married was very much against Baba, but insisted on traveling with her to Myrtle Beach.

It seemed that this insistence of his had muddled Myrna's usually clear mind. She understood very clearly that it would be important to obey even the slightest indication of Baba's wishes, yet when He smiled and told her to sit down, she remained standing, being suddenly attacked by a foolish idea that it would be more respectful to stand. Almost immediately a kind of haze seemed to intervene between her and Baba, and she was unable to see Him clearly. She gave Him a scarf that she had knitted for Him, but still the haze remained. Her future husband was called in and was distinctly rude to Baba, and when Myrna finally left Baba she was in a complete turmoil, although the love was still strong.

She was in such misery that when she went to see Mehera and Mani at the Guest House, she could not hold back her suffering, and, weeping, told them what had happened. They were, of course, kind and loving. When, later on, Baba returned to the Guest House, Mehera, who had been most touched by the story, asked Baba if He would do something about it.

Baba, who never refused Mehera's requests, promised her that one day Myrna should receive more than anyone else who had visited the Center that day.

In spite of this difficult experience, Myrna's love continued to grow; and some years later at the New York Hotel Delmonico, when Baba gave an opportunity for people to meet Him, she seized the chance, hoping this time to see the Beloved One clearly. But no; again the face was veiled from her.

Myrna married and had four children. Her husband was very much against Baba, and the children seemingly did not care either way, but nothing seemed to stop the growth of Myrna's love. It never became just an intellectual thing, and when I saw her just before her death—caused by breast cancer—it was obvious that Baba had kept His word. She was filled with Baba's Love.

Prague—America

Baba's serious car accident occurred in 1952, just outside Prague, Oklahoma. I was not present at the time, having because of work planned to fly and meet the group in California; and since everyone's version is slightly different, it is better to leave that part to be written by them.

On the night of the accident, Delia telephoned me in New York, told me about it and gave me a message from Baba that He wished me to come to Prague at once. The next day I flew to Oklahoma City and arrived in the evening at Prague.

Everyone was in an upset state. Baba had been most badly injured: left leg broken, left arm broken, and His beautiful face was very battered. Mehera had received a dangerous head injury and several less important ones. Mani and Mehru had some minor injuries, while Elizabeth had some broken ribs and was severely bruised. Everyone else was upset, and no one seemed to know what to do next. Fortunately, the private hospital was a good one.

The morning after my arrival, Baba sent for me and signalled to Donkin to say why He had called me. Donkin then asked me if I knew how to exercise Baba's muscles on the right side without moving the bone structure or disturbing the left side of the body in any way. I said yes, and explained when and how I had studied this.

Donkin seemed satisfied, but Meherjee, who was in the room, said rather fiercely, "A woman can't do that; they don't know anything about it. I wouldn't let a woman touch me." Women's lib had obviously not reached India.

Baba then made me show Donkin what I had to offer. Donkin seemed satisfied, and so for half an hour three times a day I had the great privilege of working on the muscles all down the right side of Baba's body. And once a day, I did what I could for Mehera and Elizabeth.

After some time, arrangements were made to convey the invalids by plane to Myrtle Beach, where they would stay at Elizabeth Patterson's home, convalesce, and from there go to New York on the way back to India. Bad weather all over the mountains put a stop to this plan, and it was then decided to take the injured parties by motor ambulance to Myrtle Beach. Prague did its best to further the plan and produced two vehicles, one of which was certainly a hearse and the other had a most odd appearance. But in both a certain amount of comfort could be arranged, so that was the way it was.

Since I did not drive, all the work fell on Sarosh, and all night long, to help him keep awake, we sang—not very tunefully—old well-known songs such as "Daisy, Daisy, give me your answer, do," "Toot Toot Tootsie, Goodbye," and "Annie Laurie." Twice I had to smack his face. At intervals, we stopped at wayside stalls and drank truck-driver coffee, and somehow we got through the night.

As we drove towards the rising sun, a most alarming sight met our eyes. One of the back tires of Baba's ambulance was punctured, and there was on the ambulance nothing whatsoever in the way of tools—no jack, nothing whatsoever to enable the drivers to change the tire. When we arrived there was talk of putting Baba out on the road—a most distressing idea.

We then discovered why we had been told to keep a reasonable distance behind the ambulance. Our car carried everything in the way of tools, making it possible for our beloved Baba and Mehera to remain inside the ambulance and, after a short pause for repairs, continue on the way to Myrtle Beach.

Two Coats

When Baba, for the first time after World War II, announced His intention of coming to the States, among those who were greatly stirred by the idea of meeting the One whose love had already deeply touched their hearts was Tex.

He was a dancer, who was also skilled in certain handicrafts, could make clothes, shoes and had even been known to make a garden chair and build a shed.

Feeling that he must make something to give Baba on His arrival, he set to work and made a beautiful white coat. When Baba, after the motor accident in Prague, Oklahoma, and subsequent recuperation at Elizabeth's house in Myrtle Beach, visited New York, Tex was able to give Him the coat. At that time Baba simply ignored this love offering. Before leaving America, however, Baba told me to telephone Tex and said, "Tell that boy he has just put his head in a noose. When Baba needs a new coat, he is to make it and he is not to work on it until I tell him to."

At that time the fate of the white coat was unknown, but years later Mehera told Tex that it had been worn a great deal.

Time passed, and no order came for the new coat.

In 1956, news came that Baba would again visit Myrtle Beach, and again Tex, feeling a strong urge to make something for Baba, started off on some sandals. These were not finished when Baba arrived, and Tex took them to Myrtle Beach intending to finish them there. Before he was able to do this, at six o'clock one morning Baba sent for him, and after pointing out the natural charm and beauty of the Center, He suddenly and surprisingly said, "Make the coat."

Tex, instead of reacting suitably to this, told Baba of the sandals, and asked if it would not be better to finish them first. Baba turned to Eruch as if consulting him and then said, "Finish the sandals first."

This suggestion had been a mistake. Everything went wrong with the sandal enterprise. Baba did not like them, they did not fit, and poor Tex spent every spare moment correcting the errors. Finally and triumphantly, the alterations were made and Baba, to Tex's relief, accepted the gift.

The saga of the second coat shows even more trouble for Tex. First of all, at Myrtle Beach, there was no time or opportunity to do the necessary shopping; and since Tex had neither material, large scissors or anything else to create this masterpiece, he had to wait until the party reached San Francisco.

There Tex received permission to go to the shops where he found a beautiful sky blue woolen material and other necessities: needles, cotton, scissors, etc.

Again there was very little time to work on the coat and Baba filled up everyone's time by jokingly asking at intervals, "Is the coat finished?" If only there had been a sewing machine, but no, Tex had to do every stitch by hand.

At last, on the night before Baba's departure, the coat was finished and Tex was given permission to break the rules and leave the coat on Baba's doorstep at any time during the night. This he did and then, exhausted and limp, crawled thankfully to bed only to be called up very early the next morning by a knock on his door and a voice saying, "Baba wants to see you at once."

He threw on some clothes and dashed over to Baba's room, where he found Baba, His eyes shining with loving mischief, signing to ask if He looked well in the coat which He was wearing.

It fitted beautifully, but sad to relate, the pockets usually found in the lower part of Baba's coats had been omitted! Poor Tex.

And to tease him, Baba kept trying to put His hands into imaginary pockets.

He did, however, wear the coat on His departure and it looked extremely well on Him in spite of its pocketless condition.

Love Is the Key

Near the close of His 1956 trip to America, Baba with some close disciples and many persons who loved Him and lived in the neighborhood of San Francisco stayed in that city for a few days at a charming Holiday Inn. The building together with a high wall surrounded a garden which contained a small swimming pool, and it was an altogether delightful place. From there Baba made short trips to visit the homes of many of His Sufi followers who lived in the neighborhood, while other devotees came to the hotel to see Him and feel the warmth of His love.

One morning a woman came to a gate in the wall. She asked the first person she saw if it were possible for her to meet Meher Baba, adding that she felt strongly drawn to Him and it would mean much to her just to see Him.

The girl she spoke to asked rather officiously, "What group do you belong to?" She replied that she did not belong to any group, and was then told by this "know-it-all" that unless she was associated with some group it would not be possible for her to see Baba.

The woman seemed devastated and near tears. Fortunately one of Baba's mandali heard this curious interchange. He immediately stepped in and told her to wait, that he himself would tell Baba of her request to meet Him. This request Baba immediately granted.

After the meeting with Baba, a radiant-looking

woman emerged from His room, glowing and happy from her few moments in His loving presence.

Baba then sent for some of His disciples and a few of the other people who were staying in the hotel. He proceeded to ask a somewhat startled Elizabeth if she belonged to a group. She replied firmly that she belonged to no group and saw no reason for so doing. Her only wish was to serve Baba in any way indicated by Him. He then asked Kitty, me and several others the same question, and received the same kind of surprised answer.

Baba then seemed satisfied. He went on to make it clear to all that to find Him no organization was necessary but that love for Him and obedience to His slightest wish could draw one more quickly towards Him than any other way.

Baba at the first sign of a false idea poking its head out of the ground would so often quickly uproot it and replace it with a planting of Love.

A short story illustrating the way Baba dealt lovingly but in an unorthodox manner with one who did not initially seem the right type to serve Him is as follows: In a village near Meherabad there lived a man who was well known to be a skillful thief in quite a large way. He came in contact with Baba and was caught up in love for Him, and after some time showed a wish to alter his way of living.

Around this time Baba was arranging for a large gathering of people to come to Meherabad and stay within the aura of His Love. They were to sleep in tents, covered wagons, and other temporary accommodations. Baba then sent for the thief and gave him orders to see that during this gathering nothing was stolen, and put him in charge of everyone's easily movable property. Backed by his knowledge of the craft of thievery, he let no one get away with anything. Nothing disappeared. Apparently after this he restarted his life in a new and useful manner.

The Carriers

In 1958, when Baba went to Myrtle Beach, He was unable to walk very far, and to cover the long distances on foot in the Myrtle Beach Center was an impossibility for Him. He therefore used a chair that had on either side a long fixed pole running parallel to the ground and long enough to allow the chair to be lifted and carried by four persons. This enviable task Baba gave to the group of five male dancers, who took turns being the odd man out. Two in front and two behind, they lovingly and intently carried Baba in His chair to the beach and the barn and to other spots in the Center where He would go to be with the crowds, who either accompanied the chair or were awaiting Baba's arrival at a given spot.

Some of the other men in the Center tried to get their hands on a shaft, but except for the time when Baba allowed four of them to carry Him for a short distance, the dancers kept their job. And they really had to fight for it.

One of the envious ones decided that if in the early morning he could get to the chair before the regular carriers arrived, he could possibly get a shaft and with great determination stick to it. After this young man had early one morning started off towards the chair, the news of this plan reached Donald—one of the dancers—who at once, regardless of snakes and tangled, scratching and tripping undergrowth, took a shortcut straight across country to where the chair had been stabled for the night near the barn. When the young man arrived, Donald was already there to thwart his nefarious project. Almost immediately the other dancers came in sight, running to save their precious assignment. It was saved.

One day Donald, who had had more than his share of time helping to carry Baba, began to feel guilty about this, but could not make himself give the place to Tex, the odd man out. He just clung on. Suddenly Baba, although surrounded by a crowd of persons, each one hoping for a little attention, stopped the procession and indicated that Tex should have his turn.

Somehow Baba never seemed to miss anything.

Dancing for Baba

Although Baba invariably invited me to dance for Him when and where it was practically impossible to give even a mediocre performance, He treated a group of my pupils, who loved Him, very differently. First of all, they had time to prepare, to rehearse, make costumes and arrange a balanced program. Secondly, they danced in the barn at Myrtle Beach, using part of the room as an auditorium, and the other end as a stage.

They were all experienced dancers, and among them was a young French dancer, Jean Cebron, who had a gift of artistry which enabled him to allow the meaning of anything he might be dancing to come up from the depths of his being. He gave Baba his all, and immediately Baba stopped the program and made Jean sit crosslegged on the ground close to, but with his back to, Baba and for about three minutes there was a deep and pregnant silence in the barn. Baba then clapped His hands and the program went on.

The well-known choreographer Paul Taylor, although not one of Baba's followers, announced that he would like to create something for Baba and he arranged a beautiful small pas de deux for Viola Farber (who now runs her own company) and Pete Saul (now teaching.

Tex Hightower, a member of Agnes DeMille's company (now teaching), and Cathryn Damon (now a television personality) presented a couple of excellent pas de deux.

Bunty Kelly, having been a member of the Royal Ballet, remembered Ashton's enchanting skating ballet, "Les Patineurs," and that was danced with great gusto and verve by her and the rest of the company.

Perhaps for one moment in time, these young dancers came close to being the dance rather than just dancing. Only Baba's presence could have worked that miracle.

Incident at the East-West Gathering

I n 1962 at the East-West Gathering in Poona, an unforgettable and touching incident occurred. The inhabitants of a small fishing village somewhere in the neighborhood of Bombay heard of the gathering and seized the chance to go for a short time and get close to Baba. They pulled their boats high up on the beach, left their cattle with sufficient food and water for three days, took a few necessities and went by train to Poona. There, with about 3000 others, they spent some wonderful hours, looking at Baba and listening to translations of His gestures, as He sat radiant and heart-shaking on a raised platform at the end of a long tent.

They, not expecting any special attention, were contented with this experience, and on the third morning got up early and went to the station to return to their neglected animals.

One of Baba's disciples told Him of these poor people and their sacrifice to come to Him. He immediately sent someone to fetch them back from the station. He gave them a loving welcome, embraced them and asked them to sing, dance or perform for Him in any way they were able.

They seemed overcome with happiness and love, and for this wonderful Being brought out all their small accomplishments and He, after every small performance, showed great signs of pleasure, thus adding immeasurably to their dazed joy. Such poverty and such bliss.

Most of those watching this moving scene had difficulty in restraining their tears.

Bibliography

Readers who wish to know more about Meher Baba are referred to the following:

God Speaks by Meher Baba. The Theme of Creation and Its Purpose. First published in 1955. Dodd, Mead & Co., New York, 1973. Cloth.

Discourses by Meher Baba, edited by Ivy O. Duce and Don E. Stevens. These Discourses first appeared in the **Meher Baba Journals**, 1938-1942, and were later printed in India in a five-volume edition. A three-volume paperback edition was published in 1967 by Sufism Reoriented, Inc., San Francisco.

God to Man and Man to God, a one volume edition of Meher Baba's Discourses edited and condensed by C.B. Purdom. First published in England in 1955 by Victor Gollancz; reissued in 1975 by Sheriar Press. Paperback and cloth.

The Everything and the Nothing by Meher Baba. Discourses given in the late 'fifties and early 'sixties, compiled by Francis Brabazon. Available from Sheriar Press. Paperback and cloth.

The Perfect Master by C.B. Purdom. The story of Baba's life up to 1936. First published in England in 1937; reprinted in paperback by Sheriar Press, 1976.

The God-Man by C.B. Purdom. A full and rich biography of Meher Baba up to 1962. Published in England in 1964 and reprinted in 1971 by Sheriar Press. Cloth.

The Beloved: The Life and Work of Meher Baba by Naosherwan Anzar. A pictorial biography interweaving 165 photographs with a colorful text. Published in 1974 by Sheriar Press. Cloth.

Treasures from the Meher Baba Journals, compiled and edited by Jane Barry Haynes. An excellent selection from the 1938-1942 Journals including beautiful photographs of the life with Meher Baba during that period. Published in 1980 by Sheriar Press. Paperback.

There are many books by and about Meher Baba. For a free booklist or further information contact:

Sheriar Press
801 13th Avenue South
North Myrtle Beach
South Carolina 29582